Wild Comfort

Wild Comfort

The Solace of Nature

Kathleen Dean Moore

TRUMPETER

BOSTON
2010

TRUMPETER BOOKS
An imprint of Shambhala Publications, Inc.
Horticultural Hall
300 Massachusetts Avenue
Boston, Massachusetts 02115
www.shambhala.com

9 8 7 6 5 4 3 2 1

First edition
Printed in Canada

♾ This edition is printed on acid-free paper that meets the
American National Standards Institute z39.48 Standard.
♻ This book was printed on 100% postconsumer recycled paper.
For more information please visit www.shambhala.com.

Distributed in the United States by Random House, Inc.,
and in Canada by Random House of Canada Ltd

Designed by Daniel Urban-Brown

Library of Congress Cataloging-in-Publication Data
Moore, Kathleen Dean.
Wild comfort: the solace of nature / Kathleen Dean Moore.—1st
ed.
p. cm.
Includes bibliographical references.
ISBN 978-1-59030-771-7 (pbk.; alk. paper)
1. Philosophy of nature. 2. Nature—Psycholgical aspects. I. Title.
BD851.M66 2010
508—DC22
2009034550

For Dora Wood Dean and Ruth Baumann Moore

Those who contemplate the beauty of the earth find reserves of strength that will endure as long as life lasts.

—RACHEL CARSON, *A Sense of Wonder*

Contents

Introduction

This is a book about the comfort and reassurance of wet, wild places. I have felt their peace, the steady surge and flow of the sea on sand, water slipping over stones. There is meaning in the natural rhythms of dying and living, winter and spring, bones and leaves. Even in times of bewilderment or despair, there is the steadfast ground underfoot—pine duff, baked clay, stone turned red in the rain. I am trying to understand this, the power of water, air, earth, and time to bring gladness gradually from grief and to restore meaning to lives that seem empty or unmoored. This book moves from gladness to sorrow, as life often does, and climbs through what might be prayer or a kind of stillness, to restored meaning and hope, to peace, maybe even to celebration and the courage to be glad again.

I had set out to write a different book. I had begun to write about happiness. The book I planned was a sort of research project, trying to put my finger on what makes a person happy, examining in exact detail the smell of tomatoes on the vine, the surprise of an old man singing, the rising up of green fields after winter. But events overtook me. I guess that's how I'll say it. That autumn, events overtook me, death after death, and my life became an experiment in sadness. One friend drowned. Another died of Lou Gehrig's disease. My father-in-law faded away like steam from stones.

Then, on September 22, a fuel truck rounded a curve on the coast highway and ran head-on into Franz Dolp's car, killing him. He was my friend, my partner in the Spring Creek Project, and a good man, the sort of person who named his golden retriever Sunshine and carried poems in his pack. For many years, he taught economics. Eventually he quit the university, his radical compassion not quite close enough to the required curriculum, and moved into a cabin on cut-over land. There he planted ten thousand trees—cedar, hemlock, Douglas-fir. His plan was to grow an ancient forest, although he was never sure if it was the forest or himself he was hoping to redeem. We have sifted his ashes into Ten Mile Creek. The fuel truck driver was not injured in the accident, but Sunshine was so grievously hurt that she had to be shot.

I don't know what despair is, if it's something or nothing, a kind of filling up or an emptying out. I don't know what sorrow does to the world, what it adds or takes away. What I think I do know now is that sorrow is part of the Earth's great cycles, flowing into the night like cool air sinking down a river course. To feel sorrow is to float on the pulse of the Earth, the surge from living to dying, from coming into being to ceasing to exist. Maybe this is why the Earth has the power over time to wash sorrow into a deeper pool, cold and shadowed. And maybe this is why, even though sorrow never disappears, it can make a deeper connection to the currents of life and so connect, somehow, to sources of wonder and solace. I don't know.

And I don't know what gladness is or where it comes from, this splitting open of the self. It takes me by surprise. Not an awareness of beauty and mystery, but beauty and mystery themselves, flooding into a mind suddenly without boundaries. Can this be gladness, to be lifted by that flood?

Late on the night I finished this book, I felt my way to the edge of the Pacific Ocean. Clouds obscured the moon. I could hear the shifting of the dark sea but could only imagine the surge and ebb of its rim on the sand. Then the clouds slid out from under the moon. The advancing edge of waves gathered moonlight and pushed it toward land. The line of light wavered there, shaking in the wind, then slid out to sea. And so it was, up and down the beach, a rim of light riding in on the swash and slipping back into the night. I was happy then, standing in the surge with lines of moonlight catching on my rubber boots. This is something that needs explaining, how light emerges from darkness, how comfort wells up from sorrow. The Earth holds every possibility inside it, and the mystery of transformation, one thing into another. This is the wildest comfort. That's what this book is about.

KDM
CORVALLIS, OREGON

Gladness

The Solace of Snakes

The snakes have spent the winter underground, thick and torpid in dark cracks between the rocks along the railroad. They tangle together down there, sealed in by a glaze of ice. In March, Frank and I checked all the snake tins on our land, thinking that a warm week might have tricked the snakes into coming up early. Snake tins are door-sized scraps of corrugated metal roofing that we've scattered along the fencerows. Snakes shelter there in the spring, warmed by heat collected in the metal folds. On a good snake morning, lifting a snake tin can be like opening a door to the underworld and peering into its dark, bare-earth tunnels, its flickering red tongues.

That early in the season, all we found were mice and voles in nests woven with dried grass. A large vole shot out of a nest and ran in tight circles, dropping blind babies from her teats like ripe plums. Under another tin, we found the skeleton of a mouse, its neck craning awkwardly and its eye sockets watching the sky, a mouse fearful to its very bones.

But now in April the snakes are back. They must have emerged while we were away, flowing across rocks with a sound like children whispering, and gliding under alders to the tins where new mice are being born. The rubber boas always show up first, about the time when vultures return from Mexico and skunk cabbages poke through mud in the swale. When Indian plums bloom and varied thrushes begin to call, we start finding garter snakes. Gopher snakes emerge from the ground when the field strawberries bloom.

It's not just snakes that are emerging this Oregon morning. Steam rises from the creek. Blackberry shoots thrust through the soil. Barn swallows arc into warm air above the railroad, chasing midges. Rain that fell like dead weight all winter long defies gravity in the spring. Mist floats over the river and drifts away east. Even my own spirits are lifting, as if heavy snow has melted off my shoulders and I am light again. I would not be surprised to see Persephone herself crawl on her elbows from under a mat of dead grass, dirt in her hair and snakes in her hands.

On our land, farmers long ago cleared away the fallen trees and sheets of bark that might have sheltered snakes. Hard luck for the snakes, because skunks hunt the fencerows and red-tailed hawks patrol the fields. So we put tins out ten years ago, scrounging metal roofing from junk yards. This was our children's Father's Day present to Frank, to carry floppy sheets of metal on their heads across the fields, drop them into sunny places that looked vaguely snaky, traipse back for another, all day long. Then we waited impatiently for the earth under the tins to ripen. Under a good, ripe snake tin, the dirt is rich and lumpy and crawling with food. There are slugs and earthworms, grubs, fat juicy ant eggs, nests of newborn mice sometimes, and black beetles—a dark, slippery, shining, damp abundance. Voles dig a network of tunnels and are eaten for their trouble.

I check the snake tins in the morning, before the snakes leave for the hunt. The first tin is empty except for a centipede. But when I lift the next one, I'm startled by a huge coiled gopher snake. Dusty and mottled as dirt, the gopher snake lifts its tail and opens its mouth in a good-enough imitation of a rattlesnake. They'll bite if they have a chance, and even though they're not poisonous, who wants dirty fangs clamped on her thumb?

I traipse across the field to the next tin. By now robins are calling their morning songs and sunlight comes in sideways. This is usually a good tin, under the oaks at the edge of the field. I'm not disappointed. Here are a garter snake and three little boas in a pile. I don't bother the garter snake. It will try to bite, but that's not the worst of it. Pick up a garter snake and it will force its way through the cracks between your fingers; your fingers are not strong enough to resist that push. You will find yourself pouring a snake from one hand into the other and back again. Once you put the snake down, you will discover that your hands are marked by brown snake-stain with a smell you can't wash off—like skunk, but not so lemony. More like dog manure.

But the rubber boas! Soon I am cradling a boa in cupped hands. The temptation to caress a rubber boa is almost overwhelming—its skin is so clean, its darting tongue just a tickle, its little lips pitted with warmth sensors, its eyes like flakes of gold no bigger than the head of a pin. Even the females, the biggest ones, are barely two feet long—brown on top, yellow on their bellies, and uniformly thick for their entire length, so they look like gingerbread dough pushed out the big hole of a cookie press into long, looping piles. Their tongues are red and forked. When a tongue flicks out, it gathers molecules from the air. When it flicks in, each tine of the fork sticks into its own little pit on the top of the snake's mouth, and the essence of the air surges straight into its little brain—not tasting, not smelling, but in another way directly knowing the acid of adult eagerness or the sweet milky warmth of the morning.

You can scoop a boa into your hands and it will sit there in a pile, until your blood warms its muscles and it uncoils almost imperceptibly and winds itself smoothly around your wrist. Sometimes the prehensile tail will grope over your hand and grip one finger, like small children do. Then you can sit with your back to the spring sun and cradle a snake in your hands and rejoice quietly, and the snake will settle into the warmth and stillness.

Snake-tin survey: April 7. Clear, 62 degrees. 10 AM.
1. Nothing.
2. A stub-tailed gopher snake, 2 feet long.
3. Small garter snake and 3 rubber boas.
4. Alligator lizard, 10 inches.
5. Nothing.
6. Nothing.
7. 1 small dark rubber boa.
8. Garter snake.
9. 4 nice rubber boas.
10. Nothing (except that a white trillium is blooming over by the seed spreader).
11. 1 Oregon vole.
12. 1 small rubber boa, starting to shed.
13. Nothing.
14. 2 baby garter snakes, 6 inches long.
15. Nothing under the board (but a baby garter snake nearby).

I would like to sit all day and night by the side of a snake tin and watch the comings and goings. Who arrives at the snake tin? Who leaves? On what mission? Are there sexual liaisons?

Are there meetings of the minds? I would sit quietly and watch the gathering, the way an unseen child on the staircase looks between the bars of the banisters onto the urgings and stirrings of the grown-ups. I wouldn't be a pest. I just want to watch.

But this is stupid, I know, because I can't see in the dark, and my mind can't discern what moves the snakes. Scientists surmise that a snake, like a mouse, has more than five hundred genes in its "vomeronasal" system, this sensory system that somehow reads the air. The genes encode the receptors, the chemical streambed that carries the dark world into a snake's centers of fear, lust, hunger, thirst, and satisfaction. The human mind has that many vomeronasal genes too, five hundred. But all but six of them are broken and degenerate. I can hardly bear to think of this loss: Four hundred ninety-four ways to drink in the world are lost to us, crumpled in our exalted minds.

Humans still have rudimentary sensing organs tucked into their brains, Jacobson's organ. But they are withered and useless, the remains of the vomeronasal system that still sends messages from the snake's tongue to its brain—withered and useless, like the two rudimentary leg bones tucked under a boa's skin, left over from the time its ancestors scuttled like lizards. Now humans can no more sense the full meaning of the air than snakes can walk. If I were to sit in damp grass in the dark, I could only listen, mourn this terrible loss, and breathe deeply of what is left to me of the world.

In Manitoba, there are limestone caverns where huge numbers of garter snakes spend the winter—tens of thousands of garter snakes. Frank's colleague, a herpetologist, travels there each spring, when the snakes emerge. He says that when you stand knee-deep in snakes, and snakes are moving all around you, what you notice most is the noise. It's a big noise, a rushing noise like a waterfall, but rough-edged, like sandpaper, and it doesn't stop. It fills your head and makes your fingertips buzz with sound. And when the snakes are all tangled up in love-making masses, the crows flock in. A crow will hop up to a snake, peck her suddenly in the side, and pull out her liver. Then male snakes crowd around and try to mate with the new opening, thrusting in whichever of their two little penises is closest to the cool, bloody hole.

My god, it's as if the snakes were Prometheus in chains, spread-eagled on limestone rocks while an eagle eternally tears at his liver. The gods had ordered Prometheus's brother to give powerful gifts to all the animals. To the eagles, he gave talons. To the wolves, strong teeth. To the bears, thick fur. To the snakes, fangs. But Epimetheus never thought ahead, and by the time he got to the last of the animals—soft, cringing, naked human beings—there were no gifts left to give. It fell to Prometheus to bestow humans' one holy power—fire. Of course the gods punished him. But what if Prometheus had given us a vomeronasal system instead? What would we then understand?

In the Greek city of Delphi, there is said to have been a marble temple where great numbers of snakes spent the night. In the center of the temple floor was a hole. Each day, legend says, the snakes slid down the hole and crawled around the underworld, where they gathered up the great truths that we can no longer understand—the truths of the past and of the future, how to raise the dead, and how to heal the sick. When night came, they crawled from the hole, their bellies smooth against cool stone, and gathered in heaps on the temple floor, whispering to each other. All night they whispered with their flickering tongues. People passing by could hear the hiss of their voices but couldn't make out their words.

One night, Queen Hecuba left her daughter Cassandra alone in the temple. The small girl, her skin golden in moonlight, lay still among the glossy snakes, listening as only a child can listen, and learned the great truths that the snakes had brought up from the underworld. What, I want to know, did they tell her?

Maybe this: that there was a time when humans could breathe love and danger, when we could breathe the shape of strawberries and the presence of children, when we could breathe lions and sweet tubers, when the whole effervescent world poured into our consciousness like music. If the snakes' story is of this loss, I'm not surprised that Cassandra stood by the city gates and tore her hair and howled.

Or maybe the snakes taught Cassandra the importance of backward-pointing teeth, to keep dying mice from crawling out of her throat. Or maybe they taught her the secrets of constriction: Hold on tight. Swallow everything whole. Or, do not be surprised when your skin itches and you want to be shed of it—maybe this. Snakes, licking a child's ears clean and closing her eyes. Snakes, with their soft flanks, smoothing the hair off her forehead. Whispering. Listen: You cannot make your own warmth. You must go to warmth, you must accept it. The fires long ago went out in Hades. The underworld is damp and cold. Whispering. Hide your head under the coils of your body and stick out your tail; better to have your tail bitten off than your head. Whispering. You once were as wise as a snake. You have forgotten so much more than you know.

But the cells hold their memories.

Do not be surprised that the return of the light lifts your spirits. Do not be surprised that warmth on your back calms you and makes you glad. Feel your spirits lift as the sun rises higher in the sky: this is part of you, this snaky gladness, part of who you have been for a million years. Find the warm places; do not expect them to come to you. When you find them, stay there and be still. Be still and watchful. In this quiet, taste the air. Lick up the taste of it. Listen. Listen with the full length of your body against the ground.

Burning Garbage on an Incoming Tide

We burned trash at our Alaska cabin yesterday. It was a terrible mess, but what else were we going to do? Here in the wilderness, there's no garbage collection, no landfill, and even if we wanted to bury our refuse, grizzly bears would dig it up and come around looking for more. We could spend hundreds of dollars to bring out a diesel-powered barge to pick up our garbage and haul it a hundred miles to a landfill in Juneau, but would this put less smoke in the air? So burn we do, right on an expansive mudflat at low tide.

Obviously it is better not to accumulate things in the first place. But we moved into a cabin full of the previous owners' belongings—splayed toothbrushes, broken-back slippers, moldy peanut butter, and rotted lumber from the stairs that fell off under last winter's snow. We heaped it all on a pile of firewood in the mud. Climbing the hill to the cabin again and again, we carried down a broken table, stray rope, candle ends, mildewed magazines, until the pyre was higher than our heads, a teepee of old lumber and used-up stuff.

Frank poured kerosene over the pile and lit it. Kerosene starts slowly, but once it gets going, it burns hot. Black smoke poured out of the flames. The fire snapped, shot out sparks, and shifted into itself. Scraps of *National Geographic* floated over the mudflat, their colors gone black and white.

When the fire was sucking air and roaring, we heaved a mildewed green velour armchair onto the flames. It was slow to catch at first, fire just charring at the edges. Then it exploded into flames that raced up the arms and engulfed the back, dripping spirals of smoke, shooting out sheets of fire, collapsing off the pyre. With a wet oar, Frank levered it back onto the flames. Finally it fell through the fire and melted into a black puddle studded with nuts and bolts.

For hours, the fire burned. The flames were so hot they heated the air over the fire to the consistency of water, wavy and brilliant. On the mountains across the inlet, snowfields shimmered. Frank and I stood far away, trying not to take the poisonous smoke into our lungs. We scrunched up our faces, as if holding our mouths tight would keep the toxins out. We felt terrible, and even worse when ravens flew in through the column of smoke and began to stalk around the fire, pecking at embers. All this time, the tide moved imperceptibly in, until it was sizzling at the edge of the ashes. Then it crept into the fire and slowly flooded through, pushing a line of soot.

From logs smoldering under the tide, bubbles the size of Ping-Pong balls bobbed to the surface. For a time they floated there, half-domes on the scum. When they finally popped, they let loose puffs of gray smoke.

We slogged to shore in our rubber boots. Even then, when we looked back, there were big gray bubbles puttering up from the cove—smoke backfiring in random bursts from the sea, puffing smoke alongside a floating crab carapace and a long frond of bullwhip kelp.

I don't think garbage is quite what my friend Hank has in mind, but it helps me make sense of the ideas he's been writing to me about. Hank spent the week with a Buddhist monk, tenting on the outer shores of the island, where North Pacific storms lash in and where, when the sun breaks through, the strand and the sea and the gulls and the beach grass all shine the same silver. Hank is a lanky, tousle-headed Alaskan who knows not to surf a skiff onto a beach or pitch his tent on bear tracks. He and his little family live in a cabin they built from yellow cedar. It's tucked into the forest behind a potato patch heaped with seaweed that Hank pitch-forked from the beach.

As they walked the tide line, the monk told him that everything we notice, everything we think, all the feelings we accumulate don't just disappear when we get done with them. They lie submerged below the surface of our lives—anger, gratitude, beer advertisements, pride, gladness, the smell of the woodshed, dreams of revenge, the sour taste of shame. They bubble up at times we can't control, nourishing or nasty.

So be careful about what you store up, he said. Don't collect the bad stuff, and don't let anybody else leave their trash with you either. Let it flow on through, in one door, out the other, like a scouring tide.

But how do you keep the bad stuff from lodging in every corner of your mind, I asked Hank. Pay attention to the present moment, he said. Every moment we are wondering at the path of wind across the water or smiling to see a dog rest in the sun, we are not rehearsing our misfortunes. Every moment we are glad for the twilight of morning, we are not vexed. It is impossible to be at the same time grateful and spiteful. Breathe: sea-wind, kelp-brine, cold. Notice: fireweed, otter track, foxglove, fog, a face flickering in the fire.

This is surely good advice, but I don't know how to follow it. We are creatures endowed with the capacity to worry—isn't this one of the gifts of the imagination? If a person can hope, she can be disappointed. If she can try, she can fail. If she can love, she can grieve loss. If she can project her thoughts into the future, she can even smell the end of the world—the sweetness of melt-water and the stink of burning insulation.

I waded back into the cove. A smoldering log was floating in on the tide. I was worried it would set the grass on fire, so I stomped on the log to sink it. A string of greasy gray bubbles rose and popped. Ashes made a bathtub ring on my rubber boots.

It was oddly dark at the cove the next morning. And cold: I wrestled on a layer of fleece clothes before I left my sleeping bag. When I came down the stairs, there was Frank, reading by the fire, twisting his book to let the flames illuminate the page.

The marine radio was on: rain and wind, temperatures drop-ping below fifty, wind dying by afternoon. But I already knew this. All I had to do was look out the window. Young eagles struggled to land in the trees but missed their branches and tum-bled down, catching themselves on frantic wings. The morning light was brown, like an old bruise, yellow light through purple clouds. Such a surprise and disappointment, to expect a silver morning and find it brown. The small birds had disappeared ex-cept for one hummingbird that zipped to the feeder, gulped, and fled.

I had gone to sleep the night before reading Hank's letter by flashlight. Even so, I awoke on and off all night. Had I turned to the window, I would have seen the shine of the cove and the

Wild Comfort

island lit from behind by the aurora lights of a fish buyer's boat. But no. All night my mind beat itself up over every mistake I've made, roiled with every injury I've inflicted or imagined, every fear of the worst outcome to every decision my children will ever make—so I woke up exhausted and aching.

The door to the woodstove squealed as Frank reached in to stir the fire. I backed my soreness against its warmth. I felt like an old woman, which would have been all right, except I was the wrong old woman. When the time comes, I want to be the woman Hank wrote about. She was a regular old plaid-jacketed Alaskan until she began losing her capacities. She lost the ability to balance. She lost access to her memories. Her hair fell out. One by one, the capacities that we think are essential dropped away, until she was stripped of all conscious thought and intention, leaving only the transparency of her inner mind. But what she had stored there, through all a lifetime, was radiant. Hank says that when they sat together, watching rain roll down the window, what ballooned from her was glass-clear gladness. That's what she had left. That's what she had become.

How does a person do that? This is what I need to know.

In the afternoon, Frank and I fished for halibut. With two small fish in the boat, we were headed back to the cabin. Frank had just brought the skiff around the point and opened it to full throttle, so we were moving fast when I shouted to him.

"There's something wrong with that water."

He slowed down to see what I was pointing at. Only fifty feet ahead, a large ring disturbed the water. Inside the ring, the water was rising into a dome.

"Stop! That water's not right."

Inside the circle, herring started jumping for their lives. Then straight up through the dome rose humpback whales, enormous and powerful, like a space shuttle launch, like a school bus launch, seven or eight, I don't know how many, my god, the pressure wave! Their huge mouths gaped open. Water flooded off their flanks.

"Back up!" and Frank found the gear.

The whales toppled and fell.

Beaten by the roiled water, we ground backward as fast as the boat would go. I heard a sound that I had never heard before—a roar like trumpeting elephants. Then the whales were back, diving and dodging in a confusion of black backs and white water, as they crashed after the broken and fleeing fish. Gulls shrieked down to snatch wounded herring that the whales left behind.

Has a Buddhist monk ever seen this? The giant rising up of what had been hidden?

At low tide, I came out with a bucket to pick up what the outgoing tide had left of our fire. The cinders had floated out to sea, leaving a blackened circle of charcoal ringed by the footprints of a young bear. Every sort of rusted nail and metal attachment was scattered across the cinders. I picked up bent nails beyond counting, flaking springs, bolts with the nuts crusted on them. They'd been submerged not twenty-four hours and already they were bright orange with rust. I raked through the cinders. Spice-jar lid, carpet tacks, washers, a bent Band-Aid tin, more bent nails: They all went in the bucket. We will dump them out to sea, where the seafloor is a thousand feet submerged and saltwater will make quick work of the metal. "Out of sight, out of mind," one could say, and that would be a lie.

In my bunk, hiding my eyes from Frank's headlamp, I listened to him read aloud about drift-netters that fish the waters in the North Pacific. It's all I can think about, lying in the dark long after Frank has turned off the light and gone to sleep. Drift-netters work ships that have a giant roller on the stern to pull in nets that might be more than a mile long. Sometimes those nets tear loose, snagging on a reef or bursting their ropes in a gale. Then they float unmoored, entangling fish and seabirds that rot in their meshes. Ghost fishing, they call it: 639 miles of lost net in the North Pacific alone each year, Frank read, and in one mile-long net, seventy-five new-caught salmon, as many rotted ones, and ninety-nine seabirds.

I turn restlessly in my bunk, trying to sleep. But the image of ghost fishing will not leave my mind. A net cut loose from a sinking ship sways unmoored, hanging from a line of buoys pushed by an east wind. Wary in the night, a school of silver salmon approaches the net. A salmon nudges into the mesh. Her head slides through, but her belly is too wide to pass. When she backs away, her gill plates snag on the net. The fibers dig into the soft red tissue under the gill plate, deeper as the salmon tugs to get away. She struggles until she bleeds to death, hanging by her head, caught by gill plates bright and round as the moon, cratered with the moon's shadowed seas. More salmon nudge into the net, flashing as they struggle to escape. Currents of blood flow on the tide.

Diving for capelin, a marbled murrelet wings through the water, encased in silver bubbles. Its wings tangle and break in the mesh. A puffin hangs by its neck. The net slowly sinks, dragged down by the weight of the dead and dying, until it settles, swaying, on the dark seafloor.

A Dungeness crab sidles in, feeling with a pincer for the salmon's eyes. A small sculpin thrusts its spiked head into the softening gills and eats. The flesh fades and rots, the decay releasing bubbles that cling to the net. Soon the water shimmers with sea fleas and shrimp eating the organs under the silver skin, frothing from their jaws as they nibble around the bones. Then there is no flesh, only skeletons and strips of white skin, swaying in a net outlined in silver bubbles.

Without the heavy flesh, the net rises again on its buoys. Skeletons flap their ghost tails. Strips of skin sway. The net drifts on the tide in its glittering skirts, gathering bones, bones. A giant halibut watches with bulging eyes. Rusted nails rain down, and a hideous melted toothbrush, like a white worm. As the halibut opens its mouth and rises to meet the worm, the halibut's eyes explode in twin flashes of yellow light, and two columns of smoke sizzle upward. Whales slam their tails, stunning swarming toothbrushes, then leap on them, openmouthed. Caught in the waves, moonlight dives deep in the sea, bubbles up, slams down again, rebounds in great arcs, and the whale roars. A glittering spray of scales slowly sinks. A kelp crab with a pointed prow scratches its claw at a knot in the net. Bubbles pop from its mouth and stream toward the moon.

I wake up furious—at myself, at my complete failure as a mindful person, at the traitorous sleeping bag tangled around my neck. Across the inlet, a full moon trudges through the mountain pass over the shoulder of Simpson Peak. The black silhouette of the mountain is drawn in golden light reflected from snowfields on the hidden side. Fresh wind pebbles the path of moonlight across the inlet. From the open window, I can feel the same soft wind on my face.

Hank once told me that if I am to live this close to the wilderness, I will need to accept its gifts. At that time, I was living in a cabin near his. Anya and Linnea, his wife and tiny daughter, often brought me food. There was venison pizza and a jar of wild strawberry jam. Smoked salmon on pasta. Homemade bread. A bowl of highbush cranberries. Finally, I said, "Hank,

I can't accept any more of these beautiful gifts. I have no way to give them back."

He addressed me quite sternly. "Then you will have to *learn* to accept gifts," he said, "and a good way to learn is to practice."

I was so surprised.

But I practiced that evening, receiving a russet potato dug fresh from the ground by a little girl in red boots. I practiced that night on the scent of sea-fug as the tide sidled up the salt creek. When rain awakened me, there was the weft and warp of willow leaves on the window.

And now this moonlight, and this trembling path across the water.

The Earth offers gift after gift—life and the living of it, light and the return of it, the growing things, the roaring things, fire and nightmares, falling water and the wisdom of friends, forgiveness. My god, the gift of forgiveness, time, and the scouring tides. How does one accept gifts as great as these and hold them in the mind?

Failing to notice a gift dishonors it, and deflects the love of the giver. That's what's wrong with living a careless life, storing up sorrow, waking up regretful, walking unaware. But to turn the gift in your hands, to say, this is wonderful and beautiful, this is a great gift—this honors the gift and the giver of it. Maybe this is what Hank has been trying to make me understand: Notice the gift. Be astonished at it. Be glad for it, care about it. Keep it in mind. This is the greatest gift a person can give in return.

"This is your work," my friend told me, "which is work of substance and prayer and mad attentiveness, which is the real deal, which is why we are here."

The Happy Basket

Is that what you really want, or did nobody ask you?
—LIBBY RODERICK

I embarked on an experiment this year. On January 1, I put a basket on my desk, and every time I found myself really happy—happy in that deep-down, exhaling, head-back way—I jotted down on a little slip of paper what I was doing at that time and threw the paper into the basket. My plan was that at the end of the year (I pictured myself home alone, maybe on a cloudy winter day with the lamps on and the furnace sighing), I would spread the papers across the dining room table and study them. I imagined what that would be, to read them all, remembering. I would arrange them in piles by whatever categories suggested themselves—time, place, companions, activity, degrees of temperature, sobriety, or sunlight. This would be important data.

So many people are telling me what should make me happy. Buy a cute new car. Be thin. Get promoted or honored or given a raise. Travel: Baja! Belize! Finish the laundry. The voices may or may not be my own; they are so insistent that I can't distinguish them from the ringing in my ears. Maybe they are the voices of my mother and father, long dead and well intended, wanting only that I would be happy. Or my husband Frank, fully alive but ditto in all other respects. My colleagues. Maybe they're the voices of advertisers, popular songwriters, even the president. Most of the time, I don't even think about making choices, plowing through my life as if I were pulled by a mule.

I wanted to think about this for myself. I wanted to spend some time—no, not *spend*. I wanted to create some time to think about happiness on a quiet winter day, with data. I thought that if I could see the haphazard heaps of happiness, I could come to understand something about what I should do. Be glad and grateful, for one thing. Absolutely. But more than that: If I knew what made me really happy, I could leave behind the false starts and destructive agendas and organize my life in a better way. I could lead an intentional life. I could resist being distracted by people who would sell me happiness, or give it to me in tiny pellets when I pushed whatever lever they thought needed pushing. It would be time well spent, I thought, shuffling these moments in my hands, lining them up on the table.

The first decision was about the basket itself, the shape and substance of it. I considered a basket my son Jonathan had made of tule reeds, a swaybacked arrangement woven of his love for damp places that smell of fish. But it would prejudice my experiment, I decided, to use this basket. I considered the tea box my daughter Erin made for me of balsa wood beautifully fitted and painted yellow. "May you find peace and contentment at the bottom of your cup," the lid says, and so I dismissed this possibility too. I wanted the result of my experiment to be a surprise.

I settled on a pink Easter basket, picked out the last shreds of plastic grass, and put it on my desk.

I thought it was worth a try for a year.

So here I am, eight months later, four months before the experiment is to end, hugely tempted to take a peek at the early data. I think this might bias the results, like opening the oven door to take a look at the soufflé. There's an intriguing pile inside the basket: scraps of paper and folded sheets of computer-printed prose and Post-it notes. Maybe I should just pull the papers out and straighten them. I bet lots of scientists peek at their results before the experiment's over, and I want to read my happiness— it's been kind of a worthless day.

> Walked out to the bridge early in the morning. Kestrel in the maple, cow parsnips beginning to bloom. Every person I passed said, "Morning." Not "Good morning." Just "Morning!" It didn't have to be good. It was enough that it was morning. Morning! an army guy running. Morning! the lady with the cocker spaniel. Morning! a young man jogging. Morning, morning, morning, three white-haired women. Morning, morning, morning, I said back.

> Went with Frank to a program on Lou Gehrig's disease. Allen was there, in a wheelchair. A woman explained that as time went on, he would lose the power to speak, eventually able to move only his eyes. To help him communicate, they would post three columns of the things he would most likely want to say. If he wanted to say, "I love you," for example, he could move his eyes to indicate A17. The woman said that of all the things that Lou Gehrig's

disease brings, the most striking is the outpouring of love. At that, Allen started to sob. The woman explained that too, telling us that people who lose control of their muscles will cry often. "Think of how much muscle it takes to keep your crying inside you, every muscle tensed to hold in your sorrow," she said. I had never thought of that. People pulled their chairs closer to Allen, and his friend stroked his back, and there wasn't anybody muscular enough to hold in their sadness, and that was important and good.

On a morning walk. The College of Agriculture cows all have bright Day-Glo orange spots on their rumps, as if they'd sat in the paint pot. The indignity makes me laugh. But the sound of the cows ripping grass with their flat teeth—this reassures me and seems to be all the cows care about.

Went to hear Beethoven's Ninth Symphony, my friend Marlan conducting. Went alone, Frank in Denver. Couldn't keep myself from thinking what I would write for the happy basket, which made me feel like a cheater. But when the chorus kicked in at the last movement, the "Ode to Joy," and the trumpets started to sing, Marlan leaning in, wiping sweat off his forehead with the back of his tuxedo cuff without dropping the baton or pausing, and the music marching up and down again, and the sopranos impossibly high and clear and triumphant, all I could think was what a glory. If humans can do this, can do this TOGETHER, then they can do anything. You know that point in the "Ode to Joy" when you think there will be a rest and there ISN'T? It's about going on and not stopping. Thrilled by the music, thrilled by the hope, the conviction that if we can go on, can just hold on long enough to get past this point in history, just keep singing *joy,* just hold things together through this time, then maybe there is hope for the human race. If we can't, then the world can go on without us, but that would be a shame, because it would have to go on without the "Ode to Joy."

Rain, after no rain. And company for dinner, after a long time without seeing friends.

Phone message from Erin. Nothing to say, really, but she sounded content. She had had a good day. I could tell by her voice she was healthy. This makes a mother glad.

We were all piled into the drift boat on the Hoh River, Frank and I in the bow, Jon on the oars, Erin in the stern. It'd been a gentle river, clear blue gray, braiding between gravel bars and huge slash piles of flood-torn trees. Then suddenly we were between bedrock boulders. The river picked up speed, falling quickly over a series of shelves, through a boulder field. Frank and I leveled our weight and hung on; there wasn't time for life jackets. Jon pointed the bow into the current and hauled back on the oars, slipping the boat around each boulder in turn, averting catastrophe after catastrophe, dropping into standing waves that threw up the bow and splashed it down again and spit us out at the bottom of the drop. I could feel Jon's strength—my grown son on the oars—and Frank's relief—the father, trusting. In the stern, Erin whooped and pounded Jon on the head. From then on, we floated through gentle water and thin sun. There was a great blue heron and a good view of the mountains between clouds.

Class went well today. Students prepared and excited. After class, a student said thank you. It's a heady experience to have a class go well. A class is kind of a garage band, everybody pounding away on their own instruments and something new and interesting and celebratory flying into the air.

Something my student told me—that in southwestern deserts there is a giant water bug that can tell in advance when a flash flood is coming and run for the hills. This made me happy and hopeful. If giant bugs can sense impending disaster and change their behavior to avoid it, is this something human beings might also be able to do?

I'm lying on my back under ponderosa trees by Davis Lake. The layer of silky pine needles must be a foot thick, and warm. And sweet. I had gone out to look for birds, but this is better, letting them come to me. Chickadees. Juncos. Yellow-rumped warblers. Nuthatches. I can hear the lake lap in the tule reeds. I smell water and ashes. Davis Lake burned last summer, a horrific forest fire that burned for two weeks. But this patch of ponderosas was spared. I'm happy there are birds.

Frank and I held hands in bed last night, as we often do. We lay on our backs and held hands. This makes me happy, feeling the warmth and strength of him beside me.

Fresh crab.

Dreamed about Jonathan last night. He was young, maybe four or five years old, and he was sitting on this little chair. Erin was there too, and lots of other people. He might have been on a platform of some kind, maybe a stage, because our heads were all about the same height. He said, "Mom." I was talking to somebody and didn't turn to him—you know, like parents and little kids. So he said it again. "MOM." I kept on talking. He said, "MOM!" and I turned to him. He didn't say anything, but he got up out of the little chair and walked over and wrapped his arms around my neck in a big hug. I held him too, for the longest time, and even though it was just a dream, it was one of the most satisfying and peaceful moments of my life.

And now that I write this, I am wondering if it was a dream, or if it's a memory.

Got called back for a second mammogram. A common thing; shouldn't worry. But I did, of course, imagining a black river spreading like a delta over my heart. My breasts prickled and kept me awake.

Then, a week later: all okay. Frank doesn't rejoice with me; if he was happy now, he would have to admit he was worried then.

Walking up over a rise in the sand dunes. Red patches on blackbirds' shoulders, like the flames kids paint on their pickups. I have never seen them so extravagant. At the top of the rise, a blaze of reflected light and the salty, stinging smell of the sea. If I could mainline that smell, I could live like an ecstatic.

Walking fast in the morning, down the path to the bridge.

A patch of sun and a glass of wine after work.

Tired, and a load of firewood stacked in the garage. It's oak and maple that Frank and I cut at the farm: Frank cutting wood in a cloud of noise and fumes, emerging from the smoke covered with woodchips. Me darting in to pick up the logs and chuck them toward the van. Then picking them up again and rubbing off thick layers of moss and lichen, liverwort and licorice fern. The smell is so sweet, so damp and deep forest. Then splitting the wood in the driveway, the solid chunk and wood laying itself down in neat halves.

Would it be cheating to make some preliminary observations?

I'm surprised at how often ideas make me happy: a new point of view, an analogy. Movement shows up a lot—walking, especially. Contact with my grown children, no matter how tenuous—a phone call, a memory. Contact with the renewing, natural world, often through smell or sound: this is big. Music. Change from routine, or relief after a challenge. Almost all the happy moments take place in a pause, a slowing down from job and routine: this is probably an important observation. I'm surprised how many of these pleasures are solitary, and I wonder if this is my nature or my choice, or an artifact of the experimental design. In my notes, there's an odd relationship between happiness and sadness, which makes me wonder if these are opposing emotions after all, or if the opposite of happiness might be something else—meaninglessness, maybe, or emptiness. I'm sort of surprised that for eight months, there aren't more happy moments, and I wonder if I'm living my life like a flat brain wave, or if I'm just unreliable about taking notes. I don't know what a normal allotment of happiness is, I guess.

When I compare the happy basket to my calendar, I see that there is little meaningful relationship between what I put on my calendar and what I put in the happy basket. I'm reminded of all the time-heavy things that don't show up in the stack of papers. There's no mention of my promotion—*la de da*. No mention of ticking things off a to-do list. No competition for reputation, the human motivation that causes so much trouble and takes so much time and attention. There's no mention of shopping or possessing, although adequate income is a baseline firmly and invisibly supporting each entry. There's really no explicit mention of helping other people. Technology is invisibly present in the phone calls and automobiles and, in a few cases airplanes, that support these experiences, but in nowhere near the quantities proportional to the time I sink into it. Good health lurks in every entry. As for my calling, teaching shows up, but writing doesn't, and of the trappings of writing—the acceptances and invitations and kind letters—nary a one.

I'm warning myself against generalizing from my own experience, but of course that's what I'm going to do. So, okay: I would suggest that the elements of happiness might include (1) a certain baseline standard of security; (2) significant contact with the natural world, its sights and smells and sounds and comfort; (3) meaningful work; (4) family or some other set of people who love you and whom you deeply love; (5) stimulating ideas; (6) celebratory arts—and (7) the time to pause to notice these and rejoice in them.

> Walking on the headland, we found the impression where an animal had slept in a bed of iris. Mist so thick we had to take the presence of the ocean on faith.

> New-dug radishes from Denison Farm.

Suddenly, There Was with the Angel

We are camped on the empty beach of a desert island in the Sea of Cortez. It's just five of us—Frank and I, and Erin, and two friends. We have a cache of canned food piled in a sea cave in a sandstone cliff. Salsa casera, refried beans, canned peaches. Our rice and tortillas are in a cooler, which, entirely lacking in ice, is simply a way to keep ring-tailed cats out of the food. The tequila is wrapped in a jacket and stowed in the hatch of the most stable kayak, safe from all hazards—rolling stones, sun, stray lizards, pirates. We have *The Log from the Sea of Cortez*, Steinbeck; Ed Abbey's *Desert Solitaire;* and a photocopy reduction of Rachel Carson's book *The Sense of Wonder*. Plastic carboys of water, a porta-potty—we will survive until the panga that delivered us picks us up again in a week.

The sun set suddenly not long ago. First it was there, slumped on the water like an egg yolk, peppered by frigate birds settling onto Isla Pelícano for the night. Then the sun was gone as suddenly as if it had exploded, spraying yellow streamers into a wild lavender sky. The color faded, and then it was night.

Utterly night, dark and shining. There is no glow from a distant city, not an anchor light or a running light on a passing skiff, not a moon. Just black, black night, stars beyond counting, and the lustrous cell membrane of the sea. Like night-roosting gulls, we settle shoulder-to-shoulder on the high-tide rim of the long sweep of beach. The surge slides silently, invisibly up to our feet, sighs away. We can hear thuds from distant bat rays. The rays fling themselves into the air, hang there like panicked picnic tables, and thunk back into the water. There is no seeing this tonight, but we know that heavy sound.

We sit in the dark and listen. The breeze is cool, the water is warm, the tequila sharp on our throats. We lift our heads like deer, turn them like owls. Nighttime creatures we have become, moist-eyed and urgently eared. Finally, Frank says what I have been thinking.

"Does anybody else hear breathing?"

Ah. I have heard this too. Not inhaling, but rhythmically, almost explosively exhaling. Without a word, Frank and I grope for life jackets and launch the kayak.

I'm afraid of a lot of things—the suction of open cliffs and deep water, venomous sea snakes, mouse diseases, etc.—but night has always seemed friendly to me. It feels good, out on the water, warm and cool at the same time. We paddle without headlamps, sometimes with our eyes closed, balancing with our bodies, navigating in a rough sort of way by the darker mass of the cliff that forms the cove and the swell that rounds the point. When we have left the bay, we stow our paddles and let the boat float. Dark on dark on dark, the air, the water, the cliffs; darkness not so thick you could cut it with a knife, but hard and shining and glassy. It would take a stone chisel to flake the darkness of this sky.

A swell lifts and drops us. The bow slaps the water. Sparks scatter and drown. The bow sparkles again on the next swell. "Bioluminescent algae," Frank whispers. "*Pyrrophyta*, the fire plants." It's the first either of us has spoken. I nod invisibly, then smack my paddle, raising an angel's wing of sparks. We have seen this on other beaches, the light from millions of one-celled dinoflagellates. When they are disturbed, a chemical called luciferin and the enzyme luciferase pulse from their separate pockets, mix together with oxygen, and release a blue-white flash.

We are quiet again, wondering, listening, rising and falling on the azure-lightning illumination of the face of a wave and the bending reflections of countless stars.

We hear it then, the breathing, approaching off the starboard bow.

Suddenly, streaks of light splatter toward our boat. They leap from the sea and patter against the swell, thousands of them flying clear of the water. They hit the boat like pebbles, clunking and bouncing off the hull, sparking back into the sea. I duck reflexively and brace my paddle for balance, but the lights strike the paddle blade too. The sea is alive with them, plunging toward our boat. They dive and flash. In the midst of the melee, a large blur of blue light surges toward our bow. Sparks glint to the heavens. Starlight plummets onto the sea, the fallen stars, the Lucifers. Their spread wings blaze one last time, then slide under the dark waves.

The glow veers away, and the sparks fade. Sharp exhalations echo from the port side now, receding into the distance. We are left rocking on the suddenly dark sea. I can feel Frank brace a paddle to balance the boat. Somehow, I have lost my own paddle over the side. Neither of us says a word. What is there to say? I have never seen anything like this, the whole hard world come to astonishing life.

Eventually, I collect myself enough to retrieve my floating paddle and pull it across the boat. *Glory.*

Frank holds a flashlight over the side and flips the switch. The response is instantaneous. Small fish leap and carom around, knocking their heads into the boat. He flicks off the light. They vanish.

"I'd say that was a porpoise," he says, "attacking a school of sardines. When the sardines see a big bulge of bioluminescence coming toward them, I think they know to get out of the way."

And suddenly it was all the more marvelous. Not just light careening around, scudding through outer space, dropping from stars, splashing from waves, exploding from the streaming protoplasm of cells—but light running for its life. Tiny leaps of light, synapse to synapse, behind the bright eyes of fleeing fish, the bright flash of fear or the driving light of hunger. What sparks sizzle between what synapses in the microscopic spaces of a mind and in the streaming dark dome of the sky? I don't know. This is new to me. All I know is that the world has revealed itself as more wonderful than I had ever imagined.

We are in a restaurant called La Costa, the five of us having been delivered here from the desert island. We order Pacificos all around, feeling vaguely sorry for ourselves to have left the island cove, but glad enough for cold beer. I say that La Costa is a restaurant, and it is, a thatched roof over a patch of sand bordered by a ship-repair yard on one side and on the other, snarls of barbwire protecting the demolishment or construction of a concrete-block building—I honestly can't tell which. We are sitting in white plastic picnic chairs at one of maybe a dozen plastic tables. Beside us is a bar stacked with glasses, and behind that, a mirror lined with bottles of gin, rum, vodka, tequila—lots of tequila, in every shade of amber. From a precariously balanced tray, the waiter off-loads a basket of totopos, four bottles of pepper sauce, and the beer.

The sun set suddenly not long ago, that same orange globe, that same garish explosion. Now we are sitting in gathering dark, with our sandals in sand and the sea slipping up and down the beach. We can hear the thump of bass woofers in a passing car, and salsa music from a radio behind the bar. Someone is practicing the trumpet on a boat in the darkened harbor. There is a clatter and glow from the kitchen and anchor lights on the masts of sailboats moored offshore. A skiff hums in, its running lights red and green. When the lights pass, we sit comfortably in the dark.

Then suddenly, tiny white lights blink on in front of us, behind, overhead. Strings of light twinkle from the rafters and posts, glitter off the sand. The waiter presses a blue flame to the candle on our table. When he returns to his place behind the bar, light flows over the mirror, glowing silver, amber, green through the glittering bottles. As the waiter moves behind the bar, lifting beer glasses up to the lamp and wiping them with a cloth, the mirrored lights dim and flash, the glow of light through liquid, the shine of the waiter's glass. Something like moonglow radiates from our plastic table and catches in the poblano pepper sauce. The sauce fires up, rufous and speckled. Candlelight sways greenly behind five bottles of Pacifico and flares red against chipotle pepper sauce, against the ground-fire of ancho peppers.

Have I never seen candlelight before, or a bottle of chili sauce? Something has snapped the bonds of the familiar. Blue fire, sand on fire, red sun fire become green fruits, again the snapping synapses and flowing protoplasm, again the sparks—matter and energy dancing in the dark. It's no less astonishing than an onrushing porpoise. It's no less beautiful, or more easily explained.

Is candlelight caught in a beer bottle any less the star-rimmed edge of an angel's wing? The glass in the bottle is sand, fused by fire into something that still glitters. And what is sand?—black urchin spines, fallen stars, unimaginable time.

Now, back home in my ordinary little house, roof ticking under the usual spring rain, I'm thinking about sardines. To see the blue flash of sardines for the first time, to see it with new eyes— there is no escaping the wonder of it. But what if I could see the familiar world as if I had never seen it before, even if I see it every day—with that wonderment and surprise? Or see it as if I would never see it again? Then imagine the glory. I'm thinking it's a paltry sense of wonder that requires something new every day. I confess: Wonder is easy when you travel to desert islands in search of experiences you have never imagined, in search of something you have never seen before, in search of wonder, the shock of surprise. It's easy, and maybe it's cheap. It's not what the world asks of us.

To be worthy of the astonishing world, a sense of wonder will be a way of life, in every place and time, no matter how familiar: to listen in the dark of every night, to praise the mystery of every returning day, to be astonished again and again, to be grateful with an intensity that cannot be distinguished from joy.

Solace

My Old Friend, Sorrow

Hello old friend. You startled me, waiting there in fog and shadows underneath the bridge.

I remember your face.

I haven't forgotten your name, although it's been a long, long time.

Come sit in the bow of my boat. It's beamy enough to hold the weight of both of us. We'll ride the flood tide from the sand shingle through the woods and on beyond the tule reeds to the pastures where the black cows graze.

The tide will push us upstream, bending eelgrass to mark the current lines. Drowned arrow weed will point to the broadest channels and warn us when a mud bank blocks a passage. So long past summer, the reeds will be bent and broken. The seed heads will be hollow, dipping in the stream.

I have floated with you before. I should not have been surprised to find you here.

See, there, beyond the log, a young deer turns its head to watch. It shudders tail to ears, tossing drops of light. We have paddled so near that I can see sky in the deer's eyes. I look for the reflected shape of you and do not see you there.

The river doubles the world—what it is, what it appears to be, two lichened firs, two spars, two storms that will blow through soon enough. I can see them coming some miles away and hear surf boom against the storm's torn floor. Where our passing stirs the water, light splashes into overhanging limbs.

No need to paddle. We will float slowly, rotating upstream, keeping pace with what else floats—small sticks, lichen blown from trees, a tongue of hemlock needles. There are marsh wrens chipping in the reeds. When the tide swings the boat around, you will see them there to starboard, streaked brown, almost hidden. I might have thought a fire had passed across the forest floor, shreds of smoke lifting behind the branches, separating each tree from the forest. But this is not smoke, rather mist on a saltwater swale, that same lifting. That haze.

Here are spiders, saving themselves on our hull. A wayward wind maybe, a reed suddenly released, and spiders find themselves tiptoeing across water. Let us paddle to shore and let them clamber from the boat to land. There will be no drowning of spiders seeking refuge on my boat.

No need to talk.

We know each other well enough.

A friend, so suddenly passed away. So quickly gone. Another. Another. Have you any words for this pain, my quiet passenger? Let us move carefully. This much weight can swamp a boat.

Single strands of spider silk drift above the tide. They catch on the deadfall. They catch on the bow, shine in the weak sun. I feel them land gently across my face. Here, in a narrow passage through reeds, the way is draped with a thousand silken threads. If I were to steer the boat through this passage, the glistening threads would collect across your form like blown scarves, and I would finally see the shape of Sorrow, outlined in silver light.

This cedar stump has been in the river so long, it has become an island. Angelica and hair-cap moss grow on its knees, lichen in its crown. Salt tide dampens its black flank. Cutthroat trout dapple the water in its shade. A merganser flies downstream, wincing to avoid us, but is it me or is it you who frightens her?

Let's pull under the uprooted tree and snug the bow to the tall wall of roots and mud. What was life on its other side?—a tree reaching for light, a sudden wind, the torn roots, the deadened thud, and now a perch for the season's last swallows. If you're looking for life, you'll find it in the upturned root wad now, the dark, worm-carved mud, so suddenly thrown into storm light. Here are cinquefoil, bull reed, red-stem, sprouting from the mud still clenched in the roots. And here, a mound of mud, patted smooth by black paws.

Is that a cormorant perched on the next stump-island? He snaps open his wings and leaves them outstretched, as if they were hung on the line, clipped by the elbows to dry in the dusk. When we get closer, he will pull in the laundry and lift his feet restlessly—one, then the other.

Too close: we've startled him. He runs across the water and flaps away.

Now the tide has slowed and stilled, swaying the grasses under a darkening sky. A smudge of violet in the south is all that's left of the day. A white egret flaps downstream and jerks into a high perch. Tree frogs call. It's so dark I can barely make out the shore. Shadows blacken the Sitka spruce. And now the tide begins to run, the sinking sea drawing down the stream.

Time for you to paddle us home, old friend. In a flowing stream, it's the bowsman who pulls the boat through the current. With this forward movement, the sternsman can steer the boat. Put your back to it, and I will steer us past the beaver-sharp smell of mud piles, through air heavy with cedars and marsh mint, the dank Sitka forest, into the smell of the salt sea, into the cooing of pigeons under the bridge.

Dog Salmon Moon

We walk under dark hemlocks to the floodwall and look down onto a cobble beach crowded with men and boys. A couple of fishermen lean against the weight of salmon on their lines, cranking their reels as fish slash around their boots. Another fisherman stumbles backward, dragging a fish to shore. The fish arches its back and leaps furiously. Even on the stones, the salmon leaps. The man pins the fish to the ground with his knee, unsheathes a knife, and slashes the length of the fish's belly, holding it down as it trembles and bleeds. Rain falls hard, washing blood into shadows between the stones.

Frank and Jonathan are carrying fly rods and wearing chest waders, but this is no place to fish. It's not that there aren't salmon. Thousands of salmon swarm at the mouth of the creek. There isn't enough ocean to hold them all; they crowd and jostle, pushing each other half out of the water. But the milling fish have attracted too many fishermen. We walk on along the floodwall.

Gulls skid in screaming, landing on each others' backs in their eagerness. They gulp down the red skeins of eggs, then flinch and flap away. In a flurry of air and frantic calling, they swirl, wings set, and land again, gulping down intestines, the red liver. I should be alert for some lesson in the eggs stripped and swallowed. But it's too much for me—the smell of rotting fish, huge gape-eyed carcasses every which way on the beach, all the men. Gulls cry without ceasing.

On the beach below us, a boy is trying to load a pile of salmon into a garbage bag. He grabs a salmon's tail, but the fish slides out of his hand and slabbers down the cobbles. The little boy shudders, looks imploringly at his dad. He reaches small hands around the salmon's belly, but this is no use. He tries again with the tail, but it slides out of his grip. He shakes his hands in frustration and wipes them on his yellow slicker, already shiny and streaked with blood. Eyeing his dad, he puts the bag on the ground, holds it open with one hand and a little boot, and tries to push a salmon in with his other foot. The whole pile of salmon slips down the cobbles. Salmon eggs bead his boots, wings tick his hood. We all look up into the screaming of gulls.

I follow Frank and Jon down to the high-tide line, where we pick our way through planks and peeled logs tangled with eelgrass and slabs of pale, vacant-eyed fish. It's hard walking. We can barely distinguish the dead fish from the logs, pale and floating. A gull snatches at a fish and walks backward, stripping skin from the carcass. When a fisherman comes too close, the gull stalks away. It defecates into a pile of eelgrass, shakes shoulder to tail, opens its beak to the sky, and screams.

We walk past a fisherman who lays a salmon on a driftwood plank and drives an icepick through its eye to hold it in place. He slides a knife along its backbone, dividing the red flesh from membranes and ribs. Then he stops to sharpen the knife, his hands white and clotted with blood, the stone hissing, two strokes on each side of the blade. Climbing up the huge stones of the floodwall, we turn back to our truck.

Even on the road, we follow a line of eggs that dripped one by one from a hen salmon as a fisherman dragged her to his rig. A crow follows us, snatching up the eggs one after another, lifting its beak to swallow. We drive to a highway bridge where a dark stream merges with saltwater along a narrow beach. A few salmon leap offshore, but the beach is empty.

As Frank and Jonathan thread heavy lines through the guides on their fly rods, I cinch up my hood and walk over to look into the water under the bridge. Bodies of salmon litter the creek bottom, lying akilter where they died or the tide washed them. Their eye sockets are empty and their teeth are bared, as if they were growling. Water lifts in smooth waves as a school of salmon pushes up the creek. Over the pallid corpses, the salmons' flanks flicker with color—odd bars and patches of green and brown, sometimes faded red, vague and wet, exactly the colors of a streambed under alders. These are dog salmon, returning from the ocean, gathering at the mouth of the rivers, spawning and dying, or just dying, as they wait for high water.

Whoever wrote "dust to dust" never stood on this bridge, cinching his hood against the rain. A desert poet, maybe, and will we forgive his understatement? How could he have pictured these colors, maroon and brown, the glint of silver?—tide surge, dorsal fins, red alder leaves, dusky light, all fluttering. In this stream, there is no seam between life and death. Red that fades from the salmons' flesh fires their skin. Gulls peck their eyes even as their fins still twitch, and beetles creep into the darkness where their bellies melt into rotting leaves.

In this stream, there is no drift from "ashes to ashes." It's all rushing water and what water carries, immortal substance careening from egg to crow to moss to smolt to gull-cry. Not dust or ashes, but cold hard rain and the smell of moldering cedars, where small scurrying things rush death back into life. I can see it happening. Unexpectedly released, the material of life can hardly wait to shoulder its way back into something that swims upstream, or hones a knife blade, or pecks at bones between its toes.

I will say this. I am weary of ashes. In the span of a season, I have watched my student's ashes spread like oil on a stream. I have seen my neighbor's ashes blow back onto bare legs in the surf. I have held my friend's ashes in a velvet bag, weighed them in my hand.

Tide pours into the ruddy light that signals oncoming dark, and more schools of salmon stage offshore. Up to their hips in fish, Frank and Jonathan fade to black silhouettes against water that darkens from pink to blue. They strip line from their reels, heaving loops through the shadows. I slide down the bank to the beach, sit on a log, and watch as night comes on. Light gathers over the mountains across the bay. The full moon floats into darkness.

But what a strange moon, like no moon I've ever seen— not white, but red and mottled, as if the moon were shining through tannin creek water onto dead leaves faded by autumn and marked by the tracks of snails. Then it makes sense—on the night of the full eclipse, what I see is a moon overwhelmed by the shadow of the Earth. The sea slides red and shining over the rising backs of salmon. Shapes of dead fish float underwater, grotesquely bent or perfect, the empty eyes staring at the moon.

Hurry. The moon is racing through its phases. Stir the ashes into bloody water, rake them with cold fingers into rotting leaves. November already, soon to be winter. All this death must return to life in time for spring: red to red, eyeshine to eyeshine, flesh to night-black feather.

For the sea lies all about us. . . . The continents themselves dissolve and pass to the sea, in grain after grain of eroded land. . . . In its mysterious past it encompasses all the dim origins of life and receives in the end, after, it may be, many transmutations, the dead husks of that same life. For all at last return to the sea—to Oceanus, the ocean river, like the everflowing stream of time, the beginning and the end.

— RACHEL CARSON, *The Sea Around Us*

Crossing the River

Those who will not slip beneath the still surface on the
  well of grief
Turning down through its black water to the place we
  cannot breathe
Will never know the source from which we drink—
The secret water cold and clear.
  — DAVID WHYTE

I.

When Frank's father was a young man, maybe fifteen, he decided to walk across the bottom of the Sandusky River in Ohio.
He had rowed across the river, fished in it, ice-skated on it in
winter, swum in it with pretty girls. But he had never explored
the mysterious, murky bottom. Walking across a river was not
easily accomplished because the river was deep behind the dam,

and back then, there was no such thing as scuba gear. But that didn't stop him. Nothing ever really stopped this man.

Somehow he cut a hole in a galvanized tin bucket and welded in a window. Somehow he attached a long hose connected to a bicycle pump. He rounded up some friends and a rowboat, tied rocks to his feet to keep himself from floating. Then he strapped the bucket over his head and walked into the river. As he shuffled along beneath twenty feet of silty water, his friends floated above him in the rowboat—one rowing, one pumping away to keep the bucket filled with air.

I love this story, as I loved Frank's dad, and as I thought about it again, I struggled to keep myself from grinning even though I was gathered with Frank's family on a knoll overlooking the Sandusky River, to bury the ashes of that dear man.

There in the cemetery, wind charged up the riverbank, knocking shriveled leaves off the trees, tossing crows into wild flight. The crows skidded sideways, then turned and sailed downwind, flinching to avoid the fence. There was snow on the wind, rising rather than falling, wrapping white scarves around the gravestones. In a sudden gust, a garland of plastic roses pinwheeled by and lodged in a windrow of ribbons and small American flags, plastic poinsettias and poppies. Beyond the fence, flocks of geese roamed the sky over the Sandusky River, forming and reforming like the leading edge of waves on sand.

I could picture Frank's dad sitting on a rocky ledge to strap stones to his boots, a lanky kid with laughing friends gathered around. I could picture him clunking down the riverbank and down and down, until water rose over his head and the first bubble broke the clouded surface. What I can't imagine is how he felt to emerge dazed by light on the far shore—water spilling from his pockets, shoulders suddenly heavy, sodden shirttail floating. Did he wonder how light he would feel, hollow-boned as a heron, if he left behind his rock-bound boots, strode west into the wind, and never looked back? Nobody knows. The story says he just tightened the strings that held the rocks and walked back home underwater, trailing bubbles and silt.

I wish I had asked him what that felt like, but by the time I learned this story, it was too late. His mind had gone ahead of him across the river, leaving the body to follow reluctantly. He died a gradual death, Frank said: TV with the sound off, flickering screen, falling snow, streetlights through the curtains, the snowplow thumping by.

II.

My friend Jack was an oceanographer who dove in the *Alvin*, the one-man submersible, to the deepest places in the seas. What is it like, to step over the threshold into a little capsule and peer out a porthole as somebody bolts the door? I asked him. What is it like to leave the world of light and soaring gulls, the dancing seam where air gives way to water?

"At first you sink through lapis bubbles," Jack said. The color shifts to ultramarine then indigo, then utter blackness beyond the spotlights, the hull creaking and popping, the noisy fans. Finally you slow and stop beside hot water that shimmers from vents at the very bottom of the Galapagos Rift, a mile and a half under the weight of black water.

Jack said he never felt fear. What he felt, descending into nothing a man knows, was a kind of eagerness, the nerve-tightening approach to what is real and unseeen. And when he reached the deepest levels, when he finally turned off the fans and the searchlights, the sudden quiet shook him, he said, and the infinite dark.

Three years ago, Jack waded into the Rogue River for just a few more casts before dinner, and drowned. Maybe he stepped into a current-scoured hole between the rock—but how could this be, for such a sure-footed man? If water poured into his waders, I don't know how he could have saved himself. Anybody who's tried to lift a canvas bucket over the side of a boat knows the weight of water. We came together, his family and friends, to tell stories about what might have happened, but we have only stories, and the deep mystery of his dying.

A young man tried to save him. Tore off his coat and thrashed into the river, yelling. For long minutes, they grappled in the current, one getting his feet, the other losing his, slipping and going under, stumbling in the rapids, the river fast and cold, full of boulders and deep holes. Finally the younger man said, "If we keep going like this, both of us are going to die." Jack looked at him, startled, then pushed away.

The water was fifty-two degrees, and who can say whether Jack drowned or gave in to the cold. Hypothermia is a peaceful death, they say, but drowning? How the body must fight to keep from drowning—gasping for air in the engulfing waves, inhaling only water. Every bodily impulse fights against that, flailing and choking. And the spirit? I don't know. I don't know when the spirit opens itself to the river. But I can imagine the color of light inside moving water—the bubbles, like ice. The blue, like lapis. Bright lenses of light welling up and up. Then blackness and the sudden quiet where the currents still.

III.

When I was young, I waded every Sunday in Rocky River, a stream that flows through a beech-maple woods under the western approach to the Cleveland airport. Back then, my father was park naturalist at the Trailside Museum, and his job was to lead people along the water, enjoining them to poke with sticks at the green strings of algae, turn stones to find caddis fly larvae in pebble cases, sniff at the muskrat mud piles marked with pee. "Shh. Listen," he would say, and we listened: a towhee scratching, a woodpecker drumming far away.

My mother dredged knee-deep through warm water, through the pea-green smell of the river, and brought back a canvas bucket of water. Then we all pressed around to see what we could see, these mysteries drawn from a place hidden to us: I remember fairy shrimp monstrous and hairy through my mother's hand lens.

I never understood why my parents, so in love with that river, arranged that when they died, their ashes would be interred in a brick wall in their church. For whatever reason, the preacher had pushed an envelope of their ashes through a mail slot between the bricks, first my mother, then ten years later, my father. It seemed wrong to me, I told the church secretary at my father's funeral, that people who had lived so lightly and died with so few regrets, people as thin and joyous as birdsong, would now be bricked inside a chimney.

The secretary thought hard, her cheeks flushing. "There isn't much room in the wall, you know," she confided. "So only a pinch of each person goes into the chimney."

"Where is the rest of my parents?"

She looked hard at me, dropped her eyes.

"Generally, we put extra ashes in the trash cans behind the church. I suppose they go to the landfill."

The stench of cabbage rotting in the rain and the rush of crows' wings flooded my mind, the flurry of black feathers, and the calls of crows rattling over the mounds of trash. I didn't know what to think of my mother and father flying so completely away. But they would get a kick out of that, to be taken up into the body of a bird, their calcium crusting against the open spaces in the bones that lift its wings. And if they stayed for awhile in the landfill, I don't think they would mind that—just a dogleg in their journey into what my father called "the stream of living things."

That's how my father explained death when I was young. Maybe because he was the only biologist in a small town, he ended up with all the dying animals no one knew how to save. My sisters and I would take the shoebox delivered to our door and lift rags to find a droop-necked crow fallen out of a tree or a clutch of baby rabbits, their nest run over by a mower. Rabbits, nestling birds, naked possum babies: we tried to save them. We put them in a box of rags over the pilot light of the clothes drier to keep them warm and took turns dripping milk into their grimacing mouths. They died, all of them. We buried them one by one under a big maple by Rocky River.

When you die, my father told us, all the elements of your body wash into the stream of living things. Back then, I pictured Tinkertoy calcium molecules and phosphorus and all the fortified nutrients in Raisin Bran flakes tumbling down Rocky River, oxygen eddying around submerged rocks, nitrogen pouring over the lip of a rocky ford, all drifting downstream into some other life, an oak tree maybe, or gosling. "You don't cross a river to a new place when you die," he told us. "You become the river."

IV.

Frank and I stopped by Rocky River on the way to the Cleveland Airport after his father's funeral. Despite the skiff of snow, we easily found the trail leading to the Trailside Museum and from there to the stream. The days were short that late in November. Low sun cast lines across the trail. We walked along the river, past break-walls and back-eddies I still remembered.

The winter I was ten, Rocky River rose in flood between sandstone walls, lifting a carpet of sticks and dead leaves rimed with snow. It had looked like solid ground to me. There was a red ball there: I remember that. I stepped off the wall to get the ball and plunged into icy water that closed over my head. Panicked, I flailed through ice chunks and logs and finally climbed a willow. That's where I was, clinging like a chickadee to a swaying branch, when my father rescued me.

Here was the same river, low and shining like tinfoil, and the familiar shush of dried leaves on the trail, the cold-toast smell. A jet rumbled in on final approach to the airport. Another plane lifted toward the overcast. Chickadees fussed in maples. A crow called, then flapped into a hickory tree, rattling the branches. Only a few leaves dented the slick of the river, bending the reflection of bare gray trunks.

"Shh. Listen. A nuthatch."

It took a moment for my heart to stop racing, but it was Frank who had said this, not my father. I chose a skipping stone from a shale bank, turned it in my hand, leaned down, and skimmed it low and hard over the river. It skipped once, twice, then stumbled and sank. Water closed over the space where the stone had fallen through, the way the present closes over the past and leaves a river that flat, that still.

Overnight Fog in the Valley

That's what the silence meant: you're not alone.
The whole wild world pours down.
— WILLIAM STAFFORD, "ASSURANCE"

Saturday night, just the two of us. Late supper in front of the TV. Nothing much is on. Frank surfs restlessly through the channels. Each time he pushes the button, it gets worse—young drunks laughing, veiled women grieving, cartoon soldiers somersaulting from exploding tanks. The ceiling lights blaze away, the furnace cranks out heat, a TV soldier blasts fire from an AK-47. Behind the screen, the black rectangles of the windows reflect Frank's face. I watch him carefully, but I can't tell what he's thinking. November has been a tough month—his father's death after so many other deaths, the deepening winter dark. Moisture is condensing in the corners of the windowpanes, like drifts of snow. It must be a cold night out there. Forty, maybe. Maybe colder. I look at Frank.

"Let's go for a hike," I say quietly.

He clicks off the TV.

We pull on coats and drive to the deserted parking lot at the base of Bald Hill. The night is even colder than I had thought. I pull on a hat and mittens as we move out across the bridge. It's dark, November after all, but a half moon lends us enough light to see the pale arc of the trail between the fields. A week of rain has flooded the field to the east; it glints behind silhouettes of alder trees. To the west, the grass is beaten by rain into shadowy hillocks. The timbers of the old barn on the ridge stand black against a darkness starting to show some stars.

We follow the sweep of the trail through the lowlands, trying to make out the constellations. But cold wrings moisture from the air, and soon enough we are wading through the ground-fog that is flooding from the ditch. Straight overhead, stars show a sharp edge, but around us the land is softening, the hill fading out, even the moon vague around the edges. Then we are over our heads in dense fog. We can no longer see the hill or the string of lights along the eastern horizon, the hayfield, the ash swale. What we have left of the night is the ground unrolling under our feet, the smell of damp oak leaves, and footsteps crunching the gravel path.

We walk more slowly now. We don't really need to know where we're going to keep moving ahead. We don't need to see the hill in order to sense the curve of the trail along its flank. The moon has dissolved, its light stirred into the darkness. I blink away fog that beads on my eyelashes. With the vague bulk of the hill to our right and nothing at all to our left—not a barnyard light, not a hulking tree—we know well enough where we are. If our footsteps grow suddenly quiet, we will know we've left the gravel trail for the shredded bark and winter-softened grass. In this moisture, we would smell the difference between trail and bark berm and oak forest. So all we need to do is move ahead. Slowly. Listening. Paying attention to the density of the darkness and the smell of the damp.

Many years ago, our daughter climbed to the top of a neighboring hill to watch the sunset with her friend. Dusk had been beautiful, she told us. The sun sank through violet clouds in the west and the moon rose full and yellow, as they knew it would. They were comfortable on the dark hilltop, listening to crickets. Eventually, they started down, following the forest trail through tangled moon-shadows thrown across the track.

What they didn't anticipate was how quickly the fog rose that night. It poured in, thick, dark, and heavy. Before long, they might as well have been walking with their eyes closed, for all they could see. They put their hands in front of their faces to ward off branches and felt for the trail with their feet. It was an old trail in soft forest duff, and at first they could feel the depression that decades of footsteps had made between the roots. They took off their shoes and tapped with bare feet. But after a time not even their feet could tell them what was trail and what was forest floor.

Here's where she started to be afraid, Erin told us. She and her friend dropped to their knees and felt with their hands, trying to distinguish the hard-trodden trail from the soft duff under their fingertips, fir needles sifted down through sword ferns and gingerroot onto matted moss. They smelled the rotting cedar, pressed their palms against the compressed earth. This is how they found their way, finally, crawling over the dark spine of the hill, down the valley through fallen limbs and wild blackberries, patting the earth with the palms of their hands until they came, scraped and bleeding, to the road that eventually led to the gravel trail where Frank and I now walk.

And walk. The trail rises steadily up the flank of the hill. Maybe the dark is getting thinner. Here is Orion's belt, the stars fuzzy but unmistakable, the three studs and the sword. Suddenly we emerge onto a shoulder of Bald Hill, with the ground-fog below us. The moon casts the shadow of an ancient oak across the trail, a tangle of limbs and mistletoe. We stop walking to listen. The night is silent and calm. We stand for a long time in the shadow of the oak tree, listening so intently that we can hear fog drip from tiny branch tips and patter on the leaves.

A shadow sails across the path. We look up to see what has made such a shade, but how could we hope to see a dark owl against a dark sky? A twig cracks on the far side of the meadow. Frank circles his mouth with his hands and sings out, soft and low. Hoo *hoo*. From across that dark expanse of winter-dead grass, only silence answers him, just as soft, just as low: a quiet question asked of the darkness, a deeper silence in answer.

The night, the hill, the plowed uplands are black. But the moon pours light on the clouds below us. Pale colors play over their surface, flowing from pink and blue to lavender, like dawn on a northern sea. There is a wash of purple, and blue lenses sliding to rose on the slow swell of the clouds. I don't know the color of love's pure light, but it can't be any more beautiful than this.

We watch this unaccountable aurora until we're too cold to stand still. As we descend into the fog, we feel our way, step by step. I don't know any other way to move through darkness, but to put one foot ahead of the other and listen for the exact sound of our footsteps. If we have to drop to our knees sometimes and press the palms of our hands against the duff and damp of the earth, then that is what we will do.

Winter Prayer

Each tree bears the burden of snow in its own way. Standing on snowshoes, looking over the moonlit hills of the Cascade Range, I can tell the hemlocks from the firs just by the bend of their backs. The drooping leader of a mountain hemlock curls under the weight of snow. As more snow piles on its back, it spirals more tightly until it forms a head like a fiddle. After even more snow, the whole tree bends. Then the curled leader becomes a bowed head, and the tree looks like an old woman bent under a heavy cowl.

Douglas-firs collect mounds of snow on each spreading branch. This deep into winter, the heaps of snow have become a burden almost too heavy to bear. Every limb bends under this weight, hanging close to the trunk. I've always thought of the Douglas-fir as a tree that flings its arms wide, but now it holds itself tight, as if it were cowed. Slide alders, the deciduous trees that grow first after an avalanche, are a bundle of narrow sticks. Each stick on this hillside bends under a ridge of snow that builds on its curved back, splaying like a flame frozen as it folds to the wind.

To snowshoe along the trail between rows of these trees feels like walking up the aisle of a great cathedral. The trees lean under their heavy loads as if they are praying. Bent by a west wind, they all bow their heads to the east. The night sky arches overhead, lit by the full moon. It pours blue light on snowdrifts and edges the trail with purple shadow. I feel that I should be waving a censer of incense, not plodding along, flipping up rooster-tails of snow. I should be barefoot in a coarse brown robe, not dressed in every piece of fleece clothing I own, including two hats. I should be chanting.

As clouds float east, moonlight roams over snowbanks and trees half buried in snow. I shush across a drift where the snow has fallen deep and soft, and stop to listen. At least my thoughts are fitting: I am trying to think about prayer. The quiet is so intense, I can almost hear moonlight rustling through the flakes of snow. The rustling deepens to a rumble I feel in my back. It's the Amtrak train keening through the tunnel under the mountain. With a loud crack, a branch gives way under its burden of snow, and both limb and burden thud into the drift.

"Pray for us," our friends had said as their father began to fail, and I said I would, and I wanted to. But the fact is, I don't know how. I don't know how to pray, but how can I break a promise like that?

The trail enters a deep woods. The snow is softer under my shoes. I hush on. Snow settles. The moon floods the track with light. What had been hidden becomes evident—weasel tracks across the trail and light emanating from banks of snow. What had been visible disappears—tree wells and the dips and swells of the trail. I look behind to be sure of where I am. You want to be very sure of where you are when you're snowshoeing alone in the wild forest at night. The worst thing? To be lost.

Here is an open slope through a burn. Black spars emerge from the snow. From the burn, I can see in the far distance the silhouette of a little three-sided log shelter. Frank will be sitting quietly there, warmed by the wood stove, watching for me to return. We like to camp in snow. We stuff our tent, sleeping bags, and foam pads into backpacks and shuffle up the snow-mounded trail toward the Forest Service shelter. Some distance from the shelter, we trample a tent platform in the snow. We let it rest and harden while we eat lunch and play in the snow. Then we pitch the tent. Dark comes early this deep in the winter, too early to tuck ourselves into the tent for the night. So we snowshoe to the shelter for a long, warm dinner by the woodstove. Snow swirls over the roof into the shelter and sizzles out on the stove. The air smells of wood smoke and scorched mittens.

Sometimes in a winter camp, we will write blessings on pieces of paper and throw them onto the coals to send them into the night. Each paper convulses, browns, and shrinks into itself. But even then, the blessing remains, the track of the pencil still legible in raised ridges on the ash. Finally the wish catches fire and lifts away on an updraft. After only a moment in the cold air the spark winks out, and the ash drifts down again, a black fleck on the snow. I don't know if these are a kind of prayer. But how could they be, these ashes?

When I was young, I knelt by my bed to pray, every night the same words. "God bless Mommy and Daddy, and Nancy and Kathy and Sally and Pixie" (our beagle) "and make Kathy a good girl, amen." A window fan would be blowing the scent of peonies across my sweaty neck, back then in Ohio summers, and I would feel with my folded hands the presence of my mother as she sat down on the bed. Then, when I climbed onto the sheet and lay spread-eagle in the sweltering heat, spitting in the air to mist my face, I felt we all were safe. But even then, I didn't think of these words as so much a prayer as a lucky charm. And even though I was always careful to say each person's name clearly so nothing bad would happen to them, it was just something I did as a kind of protection, like touching the ground before I get on a plane.

I shush on down the trail. In a dense grove of firs, I turn on my headlamp. This frightens me, how completely the narrow beam deepens the darkness. I switch off the light and the blue night reappears. The moon lights the snow that kicks up with each step, a white puff ahead, a plume behind. I flap along the trail between rows of trees with their cold burdens. Then, somehow, I catch an edge of one snowshoe on the other and before I can untangle my feet, I'm flat on my face in the snow.

I really don't like this. There's nothing to push against in soft snow, and by the time I roll onto my back, straighten out my feet, get them under me, and push myself to standing with my poles, there's snow packed in every space between my clothes and my skin. Snow has melted against my face. Prying packed snow from under my collar, I stand still for awhile, sweating, maybe shaking a little. A dark cloud floats over the moon and is immediately outlined in gold. I smack my mittens against my knee to clear them of snow and track on.

I remember that the French philosopher Alain wrote that "prayer is when the night falls over thought." When the night falls over thought? I have seen snow fall silently from a night sky, blanketing the burrowing weasels and burned spars, burying the world's scurrying under a great hush. Maybe the forest is a prayer tonight, bent under the weight of all that winter, the whole world on its knees. Or maybe the prayer is the hush. Could I pray this way, letting the night settle onto my thoughts like snow on my shoulders, that gently? Hush. My snowshoes shuffle through the drifts. Hush: one snowshoe, then another. There is no other sound.

The trail turns down a steep hill through sparse ponderosa pines. The wind is picking up. Snow sifts from the trees, glittering in moonlight. Then the moon is hidden again by clouds and I place my feet carefully in light too dim to show me the rise and fall of the trail. More by feel than by sight, I traipse through a thicket of alders then follow the trail through a dense stand of firs.

Down the trail through the trees, I see the cabin's light, closer now. There is the glow of the lantern behind the pile of snow and a candle stuck into the snowbank to guide me in. Sparks fly from the stovepipe and swirl on a rising wind. The same gust dislodges snow from the crown of a Douglas-fir just down the trail. A limb springs up, tossing off its load of snow. The weight of that snow dislodges the drift on the next limb. That limb lifts as if it would take flight, and one after another, branches crouch in a sudden downward movement, then fly wildly up, flinging snow into the moonlight. The limbs bounce—bobbing, bird-like wings—and come to rest, barely visible through lightly falling snow. There is a long silence. Then one more limb flies up, flinging snow, startling into flight a chickadee that had taken shelter for the night.

Never Alone or Weary

to my sister

Memorial Day in the mountains. As evening came slowly on, I floated in my kayak on a small lake. The water was cold, but the air was colder; mist rose in streamers and drifted downwind. When the fog floated over me, color faded from the forest that shouldered into the lake, and I could no longer make out each pine and hemlock. Then the cattails along the shore disappeared. The silver world wrapped itself around me like a scarf suffused with light, and snow began to fall.

For some time, I could follow individual snowflakes—wet, floppy rags—as they tumbled onto the glaze of the lake and disappeared. Some flakes landed on my kayak, shone there, then melted into beads that runneled off the chine. Then the snow was shawling down, thick and heavy and obscuring. My kayak disappeared under snow, and I could feel myself disappearing too as snow built

67

up on my shoulders, the whole white sky fluttering down. Paddle stowed, I floated quietly. Sometimes a trout flipped at the surface, raising rings of lapping light. But what I want to tell you about is the brightness. The water shone like plate silver, and the fog seemed to brighten in a globe around me as I drifted downwind.

A red-winged blackbird sang from the vanished cattails. He sang *okalee* as carelessly as he would sing on a sun-filled morning. I could imagine each cattail collecting a cap of snow, imagine how, even as snow banked the fires on the blackbird's shoulders, he lifted his head and flung his music into the mist. The bird called again. Snow slanted in.

Behind the obscuring snow, someone was splitting wood—that *thunk*, too solid for echoes. A whiter spot flared in the whiteness, and I knew that someone had thrown kindling on a fire. I thought you might be setting a signal fire to show me the shore. The axe's thud and the cold fire seemed very far away.

I might have been lonely, then, except for the touch of snow on my shoulders.

"Those who dwell . . . among the beauties and mysteries of the earth," Rachel Carson believed, "are never alone or weary of life." I believe this too. Far away and hidden from people on shore, I could feel myself part of that evening, floating like duckweed on reflected storm light, floating among the memories of what I could no longer see, the lakeside meadows of corn lilies, corrugated leaves spiraling up and up, the muddy slough where we had watched a bear sway by, the lake bent under my boat. There are no edges in this world. The water, the snow, the bear, the memory of the blackbird, the urgent growth of the lily are all one beautiful, mysterious thing, and we are part of that one thing. How, then, can we ever be alone?

That's what I was thinking about, out there on the water, and how odd it was that when Rachel Carson wrote those brave, true words, she was a frail woman, dying of cancer, surely weary, surely alone in the dark on the frayed edge of the Atlantic. But maybe there was a moon that night, a waxing moon, fat and yellow. Maybe moonlight rode the leading edge of the surf at her feet, and when the surf slid back to sea, maybe the moonlight sizzled with that sound of sand on sand.

I could understand then, how the night could become part of who she was, and she part of the night; and how the strength of the sea could become her strength, its rhythms her steadied pulse, its steadfastness her courage, and its moonlight a signal fire to show her the way to a place of peace.

I thought of you, feeding sticks into the fire, watching snow disappear above the flames. Life holds many sorrows. When we walked through the hemlocks this afternoon and stopped for water in the high meadow, you told me you believe it's God who watches over you and keeps you from being alone. In terrible times, you feel God embrace you and steady you and show you the way to go on. I cried when you said you can't always tell if it's God steadying you or if it's our mother, long dead—the support you feel is that gentle and strong.

If you were here on the water, I would tell you this: I love you, and if God helps you, then I am grateful to your God, and if it's our mother, then how glad I am that she still lives somehow, and for the chance that maybe some dark night she will come to us. Sometimes I feel alone without this God, this mother. I would tell you that.

In the thick of that snow squall, a frog began to sing. It must have been a tree frog, *Hyla regilla*. Of course I couldn't see it; I couldn't see anything but snow beyond my vanished bow. But I knew that song, and I could imagine the tiny frog up to its eyes in water, snowflakes falling on a head fiery green enough to melt snow.

As long as frogs sing, I will not be lost in a squall. The song tells me where the cattails are, and the cattails mark the shore. I am sure of this much, that Earth lights these small signal fires— not *for* us, but *among* us—and we can find them if we look. If we are not afraid, if we keep our balance, if we let our anxious selves dissolve into the beauties and mysteries of the night, we will find a way to peace and assurance. Signal fires burn all over the land.

On an ocean headland two hundred miles west of these mountains, Indians used to set the entire cape ablaze as a signal fire to call the salmon home. I like to think of a line of fire racing through the grasses, leaping up when flames engulf a tree. Flames throw wild light onto clouds that press over the headland, and the clouds themselves flare pink and orange and blue, casting down colors that play over the swell. The people stand on the highest rocks and watch the sea. The headland, the clouds, the waves, the spindrift, all flicker with light that marks the opening to a river that will take the salmon to the mountains. And when the fires die and night descends again, what does a salmon see as it approaches shore? Fire licking out in low clouds, the fading slick of yellow light on the waves, the last flash of scales on the backs of salmon finning toward land through dark descending night.

May the light that reflects on water be this wild prayer. May water lift us with its unexpected strength. May we find comfort in the "repeated refrains of nature," the softly sheeting snow, the changing seasons, the return of blackbirds to the marsh. May we find strength in light that pours in under snow and laughter that breaks through tears. May we go out into the light-filled snow, among meadows in bloom, with a gratitude for life that is deep and alive. May Earth's fire burn in our hearts, and may we know ourselves part of this flame—one thing, never alone, never weary of life.

So may it be.

Winter Geese in a Green Field

I'm standing on the pig-barn path in late winter, watching an uncertain flock of geese over an Oregon field. But it's not just one flock; it's dozens of indecisive flocks. And not flocks really, but diffuse gatherings of geese, aspiring toward Vs and Ws in all quarters of the sky. Everywhere I focus my eyes, there a straggling line emerges, dividing as it grows closer into a string of black dots, the dots growing into geese.

Their up-and-down movement reminds me of a rug being shaken slow motion—a wave rippling the length of the flock, or a shiver down a dog's spine. But it's more complicated than this, more like the motion of many fly-fishing lines, slowed to the flight of geese: lines every which way, slowly unrolling to their greatest lengths, then curling back in an open arc and back again. It's like children playing crack the whip—maybe this is a better analogy—because at the farthest length, some geese always flip off and career into space to join another flock of honking geese. But imagine many lines of swirling children, because the flocks fly at different levels, then dip and join. Two lines quarter on a collision course, and just when I wince for the midair explosion, the lines pass through each other. I find I have been holding my breath.

I don't understand why the geese don't settle. Is there a farmer plowing the field where they want to land? A fox prowling the hedgerow? This could be a problem: a million geese in the air and the landing field closed. Setting their wings, a group of geese sinks, then suddenly rises, a surge pulsing through the flock. Imagine, of course, the noise, the squeaks, the wooden clanks. For a long time—a minute? ten minutes?—I stand in the falling litter of goose noise.

The movement of the flocks seems to be tending toward one huge splayed counterclockwise gyre, sucking in birds as it slowly revolves. But no: geese scatter. New orders emerge in the swirling mass. I can't read these birds. I wonder why I so badly want them to get organized.

They swirl in a huge circle, denser and darker as more flocks are captured by the centripetal force of so many birds. Stroking broadly, a few birds on the edge tip and flap into the parade, going round and round in a vortex as wide as a western grass field, stretching from wooded edge to ravine. A bird drops from the vortex, flutters it wings, and lands with a hop in the grass. The vortex takes on the shape of a tornado, and birds pour to the ground.

But just as I think they will land, all the birds rise and scatter and the flock loses its shape. I swear in frustration. My back is tired with waiting. But gradually the vortex reforms and more birds flutter down from the drooping spout, then more, then more, each revolution releasing more birds, until the ground is black with geese. Suddenly, with a tremendous whoosh of air and thunderous honking, every one of the birds lifts from the field, flapping furiously. Even so, all around the edge of the horizon, faint lines scribbled in the sky are heading this way.

Patterns merging, patterns dissolving. Huge assemblages of geese flying as if they were one thing with ragged edges, or many things, as if they were leaves fallen onto a flooded river, whirling in eddies, and sliding down sluices in the sky. As if they were trying to be sentences. No: as if they were a million dark-suited commuters running from bombs hidden in invisible trains. I find myself rigid with expectation and worry. What if they fly until they starve and drop, all those commuters and their briefcases thudding into the soggy field? I don't understand the story these geese want to tell. Skywide sweeps of memory, a thousand scattered thoughts, assumptions—they all circle just outside my vision, almost something. Then the growing line of thought lurches and breaks apart.

When I was a graduate student in philosophy, I pinned my hopes on Thomas Hobbes. He laid the truth out brick by brick in numbered propositions, a deductive system, from the nature of mathematics to the necessity of kings. The system was a city of stacked bricks so perfect it needed no mortar. Back then, I sat in brick dust and took each tower apart and put it back together again, astounded at the genius of the design, moved by its beauty. But now that I am older, my bricks all seem to be birds. No starlings that might be persuaded to line up shoulder to shoulder on a telephone wire, but geese on a day too close to spring. I can scare my stories into startled flight and watch impatiently for a pattern to emerge. But if I wanted to stack these birds like bricks, I would have to kill them first.

"Things fall apart; the center cannot hold." And not just geese. The whole damn universe might have been a single point at first, something whole and dense and utterly dark. At least that's what they say, and I have no reason to doubt it. Then all hell broke loose. Why, they do not say. Everything blew apart, spraying out, but not regularly as one might hope, or by the rules. Energy stampeded and tripped, trampling substance underfoot, then spinning and spewing, organizing into us, this moment that is *us!* until we dissolve and go spinning into whatever oblivion awaits. We look for patterns, and maybe that is commendable. We tell stories. Orion. The swan. Cassiopeia. But when I look at the sky, I don't see a beautiful woman hung upside down in a market basket, as if that made any sense anyway. I see everything and nothing, and it is all spinning apart.

What is a person to do? How are we to make any sense out of anything? Is this what it means to be human—to search and search for meaning in a world that has none? To sit in damp grass day after day, waiting for geese to somehow organize themselves into one great true sentence written in the sky? It's absurd.

I laugh out loud just as a student rides down the path on a bicycle, and I'm embarrassed. What a day this is, a rare warm day in January. A father jogs by on the path, pushing his son in a stroller. He points out the geese to the child, who looks at his father's pointing hand, not at the sky beyond it. *No, up in the sky. Look!* the father says. But the more wildly he waves his hand, the more fascinated the child is with the fingers, and what, in fact, could be more marvelous?

Why am I looking for meaning instead of looking for geese? Maybe it's not what the facts of the world point to, but the facts of the world themselves that should entrance me. A goose wing passing in front of the winter sun: first the white flare of the coming eclipse, then gleaming pinions, then the white flare of the returning sun. The sound of a goose wing flapping: almost a snort, the movement of the air is that sharp, like a whale exhaling. A goose's trailing feet: black and scaled and leathery as a lizard. The smell of geese flocking at the end of winter: time-seasoned manure and the lemon-smell of new grass, and a baby passing by, the laundry smell, that sweet.

––––––––––

> Contemplating the teeming life of the shore, we have an uneasy sense of the communication of some universal truth that lies just beyond our grasp. What is the message signaled by the hordes of diatoms, flashing their microscopic lights in the night sea? What truth is expressed by the legions of the barnacles, whitening the rocks with their habitations, each small creature . . . existing for some reason inscrutable to us—a reason that demands its presence by the billions amid the rocks and weeds of the shore? The meaning haunts and ever eludes us, and in its very pursuit we approach the ultimate mystery of Life itself.
>
> —RACHEL CARSON, *The Edge of the Sea*

A Joke My Father Liked to Tell

Silver Creek

This past February, I went by myself to a rented cabin beside a stream that flowed into Silver Creek in the foothills of Oregon's Cascade Range. It seemed I was the only person in the entire park, but what sensible person would come out in that weather? Rain. Short dark days. Crows crying *help* from high branches. Air so damp that at nightfall it grew into something white and ghostly that erased the forest and everything in it. I huddled on a bench under the eaves on the front porch. Without my stocking cap, I was cold. But the pressure of a hat hurt the big lump on the back of my head. The day before, I'd fallen off a stepstool as I reached onto the bookshelf for Dostoyevsky and smacked my skull against the hearth.

I remembered every second of that fall. "Okay so far," I had thought to myself as my foot slid off the stool. "Still okay," I thought as the back of my head bounced off a wooden chair.

"Not dead yet," as my shoulder hit the shelves. I lay for a minute or two on the floor, collecting myself, and thinking of a joke my father used to tell. A man who had fallen off a tall building waved to a friend who was looking out the twelfth-story window. "How ya doin'?" yelled the friend. The man called out an answer as he plummeted past. "Doin' fine so far."

I don't know why my father thought that was so funny. It's absurd. But of course, if the joke is absurd, so is the life of each one of us, plunging directly to our deaths, the only difference among us the height of the structure we've fallen from and the length of time we've been in the air.

Crows stopped calling at 6:40 PM, and started again at exactly 6:40 AM, a good night's sleep for a crow. In the morning, in heavy rain, I left a note telling where I'd gone and walked alone on the Trail of the Seven Falls. I did what I often do when I walk along a creek—I studied the currents as a river runner would scout a river, planning how I might bring a kayak through this stretch. Back-paddle to slow my approach to that drop, let the current take me through the chute, then swivel to face the left bank, pull hard into the side channel, lean down as the current sweeps the boat under a willow. I could do it. It's a tricky river, a technical river, but I could get a boat through. I walked along, smiling, until the whole river fell off a cliff.

This happens. A person can be walking along a river, *la de da*, listening for wrens. The river has its share of bumps along the way, but then suddenly it's just plain gone. It drops away, leaving salal branches bobbing in the stunned air.

I hurried downstream and cast my eyes over the wreckage of the river. The falling water smacked against a rock ledge, turned white, roared, and toppled. The terrible force of its falling thundered in my spine and shook the alders. When the torrent hit the black pool, it shot out in four directions. The rock face seemed to

Wild Comfort

sail up like an elevator. No wonder I reached out for the steadiness of a tree.

I should be careful about looking for lessons in rivers. Rivers fall because the rock has disappeared out from under them—that's why. The force of water falling grinds a deep place out of rock and shoves up a weir of stone—and would do, and will do whether we live or die. Rivers flow downhill. Rivers fall off cliffs. You cannot trust them. This is the way the world is. Life *is* a joke—exactly that joke, all of us falling to our deaths from the moment we are born. Where is meaning to be found in such a world—*this world*, this black rock, rock wren, heartrending world?

That morning, I had walked out of my cabin into every shade of green, one green for everything in the forest: moss green, fir green, slime-mold green, water green. But snow began to fall midmorning. By the time I got back to my cabin and threw away the note I'd left—I would not need to be rescued that day—black and white were the only two colors left in the world. New snow revealed what had been hidden: That a small fox walked by not long ago. That a mouse scuffled at the base of a pine. That I had stopped to circle something on the ground. Snow hid what had been revealed: Mud on the trail. Lovers' initials on the bench. Old leaves turned to gray.

Rio Mayo

And now, Frank and I are in Alamos, Mexico, with Erin and her husband, Chris, among the sere foothills of the Sierra Madre, floating the Rio Mayo in a rubber raft. Our guide, Armando, is on sweep oars in the stern, his binoculars and bird book on the cooler in front of him. In the distance, hecho cactus and bare-branched mesquite pile on squat stems, grazed as high as steers can crane their stringy necks. The sun fades all color to gray—steers, pickup trucks, mountains of tires, mountains of stone, pitaya cactus, brittlebush. But the river runs tight against overgrown, lavishly green banks. Mesquite in bloom casts a yellow glow on green water. White egrets and black-crowned night herons lift in such numbers that the narrow sky writhes with snaky necks, and cormorants fill the trees like glossy black fruit. The river slows around islands and delays at the edge of backwater sloughs.

That's where, from those shadows, small birds burst into color. Black in the shadows, a vermilion flycatcher shoots into the sun, dazzles red, and then drops black into shade. The green kingfisher scallops into the light—suddenly, intensely, green and blue—then lands on a shaded branch and disappears. When a kiskadee, a big flycatcher, turns its breast to the sun, its feathers flare like the sun itself.

In English, Armando calls out the names of what he sees. Tiger heron. Elegant quail. Squirrel cuckoo. They come as utter astonishments, bursts of color against the gray bajada. I didn't know the world held such birds. I didn't know the world held such colors. I didn't know that happiness and beauty are so much the same thing.

As fast as I can, I am jotting down the bird names. In her journal, Erin is listing the colors.

> The back of the wing of the night heron, so dusty gray it would be blue if you breathed on it. Pale lime. Reds: belly of the trogon, breast of the vermilion flycatcher, bug in the wash, the back of a parrot-let wing. Red that is new and young, the way green leaves are green when they are new and young. The roots of the willows in the water, surprisingly pink

(like wheat fungicide or Pepto-Bismol). Blue in the magpie-jay. Blue in the varied bunting.

We pull into a bay where horses stand in water to drink in the shade. We can smell the dry horse dust and the deep greenness of the river. It's quiet, except for the shifting horses and a call Armando thinks might be a quail. With lowered voices, we try to find words to describe this blue we have seen in the magpie-jay.

"Neon beer-sign blue."

"The blue of two hours after dark."

"You know there is no blue in the wings of a bird, the way there's red or yellow," Frank says. The blue in a bird comes from the reflective qualities of its feathers, he tells us, not from pigments. The microstructure of the blue bird's feathers—a sort of tight ribbing or corduroy—absorbs all light except blue, and this it reflects back to our eyes. That's why the blue of a jay changes when the angle of light changes, why the color is fleeting and shiny. If the feather's structure were different, the bird we see would be green or black or pastel as an oyster shell.

"If you ground up blue feathers, the color would disappear," Frank says. We try without much success to explain this to Armando, showing with our hands how we would catch a bird, pull out its feathers, shove them into a mortar, and pummel them with a pestle. But we have a translation problem, and in the face of Armando's growing alarm, we throw up our hands and settle back into our seats, listening to invisible shadow-birds sing almost like insects.

This is something to think about, the unreal blue of the magpie-jay's wings. This small fact knocks me sideways and makes me think about things a little differently. Is it a mistake to look to the world to tell us the meaning of our plummeting lives? Maybe we all have the power to shape our own structure, the structure of our metaphoric wings, what lifts us—our character maybe, call it our spirit. We all in our own ways catch the light of the world and reflect it back, and this is what is bright and surprising about a person, this rainbow shimmer created from colorless structure. Maybe there is no meaning in the world itself—no sorrow. In fact, no good or bad, beginning or end. Maybe what there is, is the individual way each of us has of transforming the world, ways to refract it, to create of it something that shimmers from our spread wings. This is our work, creating these wings and giving them color.

The magpie-jays remind me of Epictetus, the Greek Stoic philosopher. "There is nothing good or evil, save in the will," he wrote. What comes at us *is what it is*. How we feel about events, how we respond to them, how we transform them and judge them—these are our own decisions, Epictetus believed. Or maybe I would say it's a little more complicated: How we feel about events, respond to them, transform them and judge them, is a matter of the shape of our spirit, the corrugation of the feathers in our wings. And this, the shape of our spirit, our way of reflecting the world, is something we must work to create and, tend, day after day after day.

As I say, this is something I will need to think more about. But I am no longer surprised when I reread Camus's *The Stranger*: "For the first time, the first, I laid my heart open to the benign indifference of the universe. . . . [I realized] that I'd been happy, and that I was happy still."

And maybe I understand now why it thrilled me to see a cormorant perch on a kapok tree and stretch its wings into the sunlight, letting the warmth drive away the wetness and the lice from the shadow of each glossy feather. And why I watched so carefully, so joyfully, as a magpie-jay ran each of its extravagant tail feathers through its black beak, one and then another.

The Recipe for Migas

You'll need chili peppers from a stand, and really it doesn't matter what kind of peppers or what kind of stand—poblanos, serranos, jalapeños from a plywood table at a gas station crossroads outside of town or from a megagrocery with refrigerator air. Early in the morning, chop the peppers and fry them up on a camp stove set on dirt in a cottonwood wash. Clear light should be flooding into the branches, casting shadows that flow over signs left on the sand the night before—coyote droppings, the scuff marks of mice. Hang binoculars around your neck, in case a woodpecker knocks in a cottonwood snag behind the rental car. The rental car is part of the recipe, I have come to believe—the strangeness of a brand-new white Chevrolet left by a mesquite thicket where the dirt track enters the wash.

Soon steam will rise from the frying pan, and you will feel the sting in your eyes. Take care not to wipe the tears, because the pain is on your hands too. Swipe your sleeve across your face instead.

When the peppers are crisp, crack in half a dozen eggs. Kneel to stir the eggs into the peppers. Sand will stick to your knees.

While you stir, a dove calls its soft sound. The cottonwood leaves are new and sticky, so when the breeze passes through (that small wind that comes when the sun first warms the sand), the leaves flutter and so do the shadows on the wash. Wear a jacket because the air in the daytime is cool and there's an edge to the wind.

If blue corn chips are all you have, then that's what you should use, even though they make purple migas. Crumble a handful in your fist and let the pieces fall into the eggs. Three handfuls are probably enough for half a dozen eggs. Stir these in and let the eggs harden up. Then dump in salsa from the jar, probably more than you think you need. Keep stirring until the eggs are dry.

These are *migas*, the desert breakfast. "Migas" means little bits, and that seems right—the gathering of small things, the coming together of warmth and cold and birdsong on a desert morning.

Frank spoons a heap of migas onto a tin plate and hands it to me. I find a seat on the sand, where I can lean against a slab of stone in a spot of sunlight. Two tea bags hang by their strings from the branch of a paloverde. We've pulled them out of our mugs and tied them up there to keep them out of the sand. They spin in the breeze, like prayer wheels, faster than you would think in this light wind, a surprise, as if they had energy of their own. Faster and faster in one direction, then a hesitation, and slowly in the other direction, gathering speed. Sun lights them around the edges—a square of brightness, spinning.

The peppers crunch when I chew, and when I swallow, they sear my throat. This hurts. I gulp down tea, then start in again. I have heard that hot peppers cool you in a hot climate because the heat of them makes you sweat, and then, in the breeze, you catch a chill. This turns out to be sort of true, at least the sweat part. So I can understand the usefulness of the heat. But I don't understand the necessity of the pain. Why does it hurt? I ask Frank. He's a neurobiologist, and he often knows answers to questions like this.

Frank says the peppers have capsaicin, which releases Substance P, which stands for Pain. Capsaicin triggers a neural impulse that travels like falling dominoes along the length of the nerve fiber that reaches all the way to the spine. The charge sets off Substance P, an explosion of pain.

So that explains the how of it. But it doesn't explain the why. Why does heat hurt? *Why does anything have to hurt?* Why can't Substance P send some other signal? Pleasure, for example, or Purpose, or Pity. The urge for Picnics—I don't care. I just don't understand the necessity of pain in the scheme of things.

Frank says the body needs pain because it's the signal that something is wrong. "Pain motivates the body to do something about whatever causes it," he says. Then he asks a rhetorical question: "Without pain, would you know to protect a burned hand?"

So, okay, I get the necessity of a signal. But why, I want to know, does the signal have to be pain? Why couldn't a little bell go off, and the body—exquisitely attuned to *that* signal—could respond just as quickly. *Dink*/flinch: like that. Or, here, try this, I say. This is even better: The injury sends the pain signal and the body responds, but the brain is never aware of it. So there is pain, and the body does what needs to be done, but it never hurts.

And here, Frank is quiet. He leans forward in a camp chair and reaches for the binoculars underneath his jacket. He has developed a patience for questions like this. Small birds are flitting in the shadowy spaces between the cottonwood branches. Are they yellow? Warblers maybe. Maybe goldfinches. His plate balances on his lap. "Okay," he says. "It's more complicated than that."

"You have an auditory system so you can sense sounds. You have a visual system so you can sense sights. You also have a nociception system so you can sense injury."

I think about this. My body is *built* to be sensitive to pain, just as it is built to be receptive to birdsong or blue jays. Dove calls, lullabies, the beauty of yellow warblers, an oriole's breast, sun on stone, tire tracks, lizard backs, a dull ache, a hornet's sting, tearing pain—my body is a receptor, built to receive them all.

Frank goes on. "You touch a flame, your body snatches your hand away before you feel anything at all—that fast. No time to send a signal to the brain; this is all spinal cord. *Then*, next step: You sense that something is wrong. That's the hindbrain working at the top of the spinal column, a little farther away. You curl your injured hand and pull it to your chest. Then, finally, you feel pain. This is the cerebral cortex, the top layer of the brain, the part that is going to have to figure out what you are going to do next. Takes awhile, but the signal gets there."

So there *can* be unfelt pain?

"It's true that before your brain knows anything's wrong, your body responds," he says. "I suppose you could call that unfelt pain. There are brain-damaged people whose bodies respond to pain but who never feel it, and of course that's what anesthetics are all about."

Like an army of ants, so to speak, I say to him, but only *so to speak*, because I'm not a scientist and so I don't know the right words and I fall back on metaphors. But I *have* seen a busted-up anthill, and I think this may be an example of unfelt pain. Ants swarm out of the sand, spilling toxins, biting air, until the surface of the hill is roiling with distress and danger and confusion, and this sourness. You can smell the agitation of the ants, like piss.

The damaged anthill isn't aware of anything at all, of course, and the ants haven't been hurt, but the disintegration is real and all the more appalling for the mindlessness of the response.

Frank set his empty mug on the ground. When it comes to pain, he knows what he's talking about. If I press him—but only then—he will tell about being taken from home when he was five years old and quarantined a hundred miles away in a big city hospital, desperately sick with polio. Five years old. Every day, nurses came in with boiling hot heavy pads and draped them across his legs—who knows why? The heat was more than he could bear. Every day, the pain, too much for a child to bear. A little boy, this man I love, alone with his unbearable pain.

Pulling my sleeve over my hand, I pick up the bail of the tea-kettle, boiling again, and pour water into his mug. He unwinds his tea bag from the paloverde.

Here is what I really want to know, and I'm not sure a physiologist can tell me. Why does there have to be grieving in the world? I'm not talking about pain now, but all the sadness. Frank and I have seen the signs of the people who have pushed through this wash on their way north, the empty water jugs and the footprints of children. I can only barely imagine their thirst, their fear. How can I imagine all the suffering of the human condition? If that sorrow is fully felt, how can anyone bear up under that burden? And this says nothing of the damage to the natural world, the broken heart of the bulldozed land.

Do our bodies have a receptor for other people's sorrow and Earth's? Is emotional pain a necessity, a life-saving adaptation, like physical pain, that tells us something's wrong and we need to act quickly? And if it is a necessary adapatation, could we wish for a kinder signal?

Or shall we wish for unfelt sadness?

Unfelt sadness is possible I think. We can build up calluses on our hearts, rough skin that blocks out our own sorrow and prevents us from feeling the suffering of others. Maybe unfelt sorrow explains why many of us are so restless and tormented; sorrow swarms in the spine, and the bewildered mind casts about for a cure for a dismay it does not understand. But once we close our hearts to suffering, are they closed also to the perception of joy? Is emotion a door that, once closed, is closed to everything that would come in?

The alternative is for us to lay our hearts open to sorrow, to attune our senses to suffering, our own and the suffering of others. Sorrow may flood through our hearts then, but won't that same openness and acceptance let in gladness too? Maybe so. Maybe by making ourselves vulnerable to sorrow, we open ourselves also to moments of beauty and grace.

But I don't ask Frank any of this because he is following a bird he heard shuffling in the bushes. He leans down to get under an overhanging limb, picking his steps carefully among the prickly pear pads spilling from a pack-rat nest. Soon I can barely make him out, back there behind the brush. I don't understand the necessity of sadness and pain, and I don't know how this man who endured such suffering in childhood has been able to keep his heart wide open to the small things that bring him happiness. But I am beginning to think that sorrow and joy are not opposites. They flow down the same pathways to the heart.

When Frank returns—it was a California quail, he thinks, although he didn't get a good look—I dump both our plates back into the skillet and heat the migas up again. Through whatever axons or neurons, we are a man and a woman who love each other, standing in wool hats and long underwear in a desert wash in cool morning sunlight, spooning migas out of a frying pan into our mouths, wincing from the pain, swiping sweat from our foreheads, stirring tiny prayer flags into our tea.

Turning Stones

There are five good things to do with stones at the edge of water anywhere in the world: plink, skip, chuck, bounce, and turn.

Plinking requires a round, thin wafer of a rock, something shaped like a cookie, the sort of thing you'd choose if you were skipping stones. But instead of heaving it sidearm, you flip it spinning on edge into the air. The goal is to get it to enter the water at an angle so perfectly vertical that it makes this noise when it goes in—*baloop*—and raises only a blister. Any splash, and the plinker loses. You have to look long and hard to find a stone good enough to plink.

Skipping. It seems almost a miracle that a stone can be made to bounce off water. A stone—so solid and heavy that it is the definition of solid and heavy (rock-hard, stone solid, weighing five stone)—can hit a liquid, and instead of sinking like a stone, it bounces off like a shearwater or a breeze or a mayfly laying eggs. If there is a child on earth who doesn't know how to skip a stone—the sidearm stance, the angle of the body to the water—

it is important to teach her. But teach carefully, as all teaching should be done. Some years ago, I watched as one of my friends stood knee-deep in water teaching her son to skip stones, but when he crouched and winged his skipping stone, it caught her square in the forehead and felled her like Goliath.

Skipping and *chucking* are not the same. Skipping is sidearm and competitive; people place bets on skips. Chucking is underhand and absentminded. I don't know why human beings chuck stones into water. They just do. Watch a stranger come to the edge of a river. He (usually he) may stand around for a time—snap open a beer, scan the horizon. But sooner or later, he will lean over, pick up a stone, and chuck it into the stream—as if he just noticed that the stone had crawled from the river and was getting away.

Bouncing takes the right kind of beach, a beach densely and deeply covered in the round stones that pile up under basalt headlands. You'll know this beach by its sound when a breaker crashes in, the sound of a pyramid of bowling balls dislodged. If you find the most perfectly round stone on this beach, like a golf ball, and toss it over your head so it lands in the stone field, it will bounce and bounce and bounce, seeming to gather energy with each donk on the rock until finally it takes a wild, arcing leap and disappears into the sea.

Which brings us to *turning*. Here's the thing about turning stones. I have come onto many beaches full of boulders and cobbles, all black and shiny. Maybe there were cormorants and oystercatchers poking into some mussel beds. But otherwise, the beaches seemed barren of life, a disappointment. I know now that had I lifted any stone, right where the tide was sloshing, I would have found crabs—maybe a dozen dime-sized porcelain crabs running sideways as fast as they could, which is surprisingly fast, or a big red rock crab, pulling itself together, folding every claw into its own little slot so it looks exactly like a red rock, or a pile of tiny hermit crabs tucked into periwinkle shells.

This turning has to be done with exquisite care. Once I turned a stone at the Oregon coast and found a small eel, the first I had ever seen. I put the stone back in place, ran to find Frank, and when I returned to show him, I found that I had crushed the eel in two. I stood mournfully on the beach with half an eel in each hand. So now I know you have to put the stone back in exactly the right place. Just plopping the stone back down risks smashing all the creatures that live under it. And lifting only one edge of the stone is especially dangerous because all the creatures, the crabs and blennies, will try to hide under the edge against the ground, and when you close the lid, you will grind every one into the sand. So I've learned to turn only those stones I can completely lift, and then to put the stone down gently, exactly.

At low tide on a healthy seacoast, there is always some creature under a rock. I suppose many of them aren't even creatures, but left-behind eel slime or oyster spit. There are snail eggs like eyeballs on stalks. Sometimes a starfish smaller than a fingernail. Algae that look like orange paint, colonial animals like pink Christmas cactus, gooseneck barnacles with necks fleshy enough to embarrass a goose, little nudibranchs like cross-dressing garden slugs. But here it is—this wild world under every plain old rock.

There are philosophers who say that if you can't see something, it doesn't exist. Think of color, the eighteenth-century idealist George Berkeley said. If light waves reflected from an object are not caught by some eye and processed into color, the object has no color at all. If, alone on a beach, you turned your back, all the yellows and blues in the nudibranchs and the purples and oranges in the starfish would vanish. Sound, of course, is the same way. A tree falling in an empty forest makes no sound because what is sound, except the perception of waves traveling through the air? And so for everything else—not just qualities, but substance too. *Esse est percipi.* To be is to be perceived.

According to Berkeley, we would live in an oddly blinking universe that flashes into and out of existence as perceiving beings turn their heads or close their eyes or simply fail to notice—except for one thing. The whole of creation is held in God's eyes, Berkeley says. Divine attention, divine seeing and hearing and even touching (imagine the electricity of this touch) bring the world into existence and hold it there. It occurs to me that if God doesn't exist, one must suppose that the entire onus is on us to hold the world in existence by paying attention. One might need to take this responsibility seriously.

On a Mexican beach in the heat of the day, Jonathan and I went out to turn rocks. Everyone else was resting in the shade of a sun tarp, reading—a few buzzards flying, a frigate bird even higher, heat shimmering against red cliffs, the bay azure at low tide (or so the colors appeared to us). The water around our ankles was so warm we thought at first that nothing could live there. Jonathan turned a big stone and called me over: sea cucumbers, soft and brown and gently floating, hundreds of invertebrates that are dead ringers for human turds. We had read in Steinbeck's *The Log from the Sea of Cortez* that a little fish lives in the gut of the sea cucumber, swimming in and out to feed on the nutrients concentrated there. So we gave the cucumber a few pokes, but no commensal fish appeared.

Huge isopods like monstrous black pill bugs crawled under every stone. We found blobs of mucous that we couldn't figure out. Sponges? Who designs these things? When we looked toward shore, we could see the line of kayaks and the sunshade with our friends lying on towels. If a gooey blob came to this beach, the blob might think the beach was deserted, unless it happened to turn over the sunshade. There it would be stunned to find huge pink, lumpy, wiggling things, roughly tubular, with hair on one end, sort of like pink sea cucumbers reading Steinbeck.

In late afternoon, when the sun had lost its sting, we hiked into the desert to turn stones. Jonathan taught me to select a good-sized rock, the bigger the better, resting on soil, preferably next to a bush. The trick here is to look carefully. You can't be afraid to get down on hands and knees. The little lives under a desert stone look like desert stones or blown dried leaves. So if you see one of these things, he told me, think scorpion. There's sure to be a scorpion sagging sideways to fit into the narrowest cracks between the dirt and the rock—maybe pale yellow or brown or translucent, usually smaller than a paper clip. It may look dead, but touch it with a twig and its stinger arcs over its back, its pincers point straight at you, and it's up on all eight legs, ready to defend itself. If you don't find a scorpion, you might surprise a side-blotched lizard with bright blue armpits or a centipede with poison mandibles, and probably you'll find a black spider guarding eggs wrapped in swaddling clothes.

If you are a stone turner of long standing, you know two more tricks, and you know that the hidden animals have their tricks too. Once you have turned a stone on the beach, it pays to sit patiently and watch. Two blue eyes will telescope out of a lumpy red rock and look around. A periwinkle shell will raise itself on striped legs and scrabble over the sand to shelter. A hole in the ground will slowly grow blue tentacles. A piece of the sandy bottom, an entire fish-shaped section of sand, will rise and fan invisible fins. A dark speck of sand will lift and whir away. A lump on the rock will reveal itself as a chiton, armored like a knight, grazing like a cow.

Or—this happens too—the fish you are watching may slowly disappear. A flounder will do this, slowly fading from dark blue-gray to the exact mottled ivory of the sand. Flounders have three kinds of skin cells, Jon says—chromatophores that hold color, iridiphores that reflect light, and melanophores, pigment-filled cells with radiating filaments that spread like spiderwebs across a flounder's back. When the fish lies on light-colored ground, its melanophores contract, drawing all the pigment back into their cell bodies, leaving the field to the light and light-reflecting cells.

So here's the other trick. Say you are lying on your stomach on a mussel bed, looking into a tide pool. What you watch for are shadows. Sometimes, the shadow is all you will ever see of a fish or a crab. The microscopic animals that buzz around the tide pool will be invisible to you, but you can see their shadows motoring over the sand. Look a little above the shadow, in the direction of the sun. That's where you will find what you are seeking.

Plato thought these shadows are all we ever can see. We never see what is real, he taught, because what is real is unchanging and we live in a world of change. But if we are attentive, we can see the shadows of what is real, the fleeting manifestations of the unchanging, visible to us like shadow images a fire might cast onto the back wall of a cave. I can imagine Plato lying on his stomach in the tide pools at Piraeus, watching the dancing shadows of the invisible sea creatures, wondering which is real, which is illusion: the shadows, or the forms that cast the shadows, or something else, some unseen source of light. Seaweed would stain his toga and barnacles would scratch his muscled knees.

It's a vanishing, fragile world he would find under beach rocks, a world made of mucous and skin and some chitin sometimes, and saltwater, but almost never bones, and this should give us pause. Our bones let us stand up and walk on top of worlds. Bones carry our massive brains. But if we were human invertebrates, just substantial enough to bend the light, we would slink or glide or ooze under the beach rocks, skinnying between the stones, sloshing in the tide. Think then of the things we would see, think of the worlds our eyes would bring into existence and how we would yearn to understand the world above the stones. Think then how stunned and uncomprehending we would be if a force that seemed to come from another world ripped the roof off our lives. We would flinch and duck our heads to protect our weak eyes from the terrible brightness and dive for the tight dark places. Everything we thought was solid, the very substrate of our lives—gone, just like that. We look straight into the fire.

I asked a freshwater ecologist to take my philosophy students to a stream last fall. The students thought it was a little odd. But honestly, if they want to study metaphysics or epistemology— the nature of what is, or how we come to know—they could do worse than search under stones. The water was cold, and even though I had told them to bring old wading shoes, many hadn't. So they winced and slipped over the stones with their pants rolled up, stepping high in water that had only recently been snow.

This is what I wanted: a dozen blue-footed philosophy students, peering into worlds they had never imagined, leaning over a hooked, beaked, armored, spike-tailed creature that would soon split up the back and open lavender eyes that can see a hundred different angles at once. Maybe then, turning stones, they would understand how unsettling are the questions they need to ask. What is real? What is true? What is unchanging? What is beyond human understanding? Maybe one of them will find the philosopher's stone, the stone that alchemists sought all through the Middle Ages—the stone that could turn base metal into gold, or give us answers to questions that seem to have none, or sail across the water, glancing off the surface once, twice, and with a last great leap, clattering onto the gravel on the far shore.

Things with Feathers

I was drinking tea with Hank's family in their southeast Alaskan cabin, when a bird flew against the window. We heard the thud and looked up in time to see a bird falling and an oily impression of spread wings on the glass. Linnea, who was barely two years old, must have seen it too. She sat on the floor and struggled to pull on rubber boots.

"Out," she said. Her mother held open the door, and I followed them down the steps. It was a dark day, as I remember, and the trees were tall and shrouded with lichen. Linnea splashed into the puddle where the bird had fallen. Squatting down, she grabbed the bird in one hand. It must have been a sparrow, small enough that her small fingers closed around its breast. It must have been barely alive. Linnea held the bird and wouldn't let go.

"Poor bird," her mother said. "Do you think it wants a warm nest? Let's find it a place to rest." Taking Linnea's other hand, her mother led her over the moss in the forest, pointing out likely places where a bird might want to sleep.

"No," Linnea said with some heat, and held onto the bird with a tighter grip.

"Poor bird," her mother said. "Do you think it wants to find its mother?" They inspected the trees for a fork in the branches or a mossy perch where a mother bird would be likely to search for her baby.

"No," Linnea said and held on even more tightly, bringing the bird close to her face and planting a little kiss on its beak. The bird's head, sticking up out of her fist, began to wobble. Its feet, extending from the bottom of her fist, clenched. Its feathers, already rumpled, lost their gloss.

"Poor dead bird," her mother said. "Do you think it wants to find a little grave under a tree?"

"No," Linnea said.

All afternoon, she carried the bird in her fist, until finally its head fell off. Then she picked up its head and toddled around with the head in one hand and the body in the other.

Linnea never let go, even when she finally fell asleep. Her parents pried the body and the head from her hands and buried them under a spruce.

Emily Dickinson wrote that "hope is the thing with feathers / that perches in the soul." But when I think of things with feathers, I think of Linnea's bird. Hope isn't what flitters in the alders. It isn't the possibility of flight. Hope is holding on with this fierceness, even when—no, especially when—that makes no sense at all.

This is the real lesson of the legend of Pandora. When Pandora opened the forbidden box and released evils into the world, death, despair, greed, war, madness, pestilence, and betrayal dashed out as if they were feathered things, flew out shrieking like crows from a swampy night-roost, and pulled at people's hair and sent them diving into the bushes. I can imagine that Pandora slammed shut the box and looked around wildly, her heart racing. When she calmed down, I imagine that she shook the box to make sure it was empty and then opened it again, reckless mortal.

Out fluttered winged hope. Hope: how lightly it must have flown on its feathered wings, how delicately it landed on Pandora's outstretched hand. She didn't understand its horror or its blessing; maybe we can forgive her. In the end, she released the' one thing that empowers all the evils of the world. If we had no hope, nothing could harm us. We could choose to die by our own hands and by that act, frustrate all our demons. But hope empowers also all the good in the world. Hope keeps us alive, even as we all move toward inevitable death. This is essential. To hold on, fiercely to hold on, even if we believe we are condemned to "a life without consolation," is the one triumph open to us. In the end, the fact of life so fully seized becomes the consolation.

The French existentialist Albert Camus compared hope to the painted screen that executioners once held in front of the faces of prisoners to hide their view of the scaffold as they climbed the stairs. Instead of black crows hunched on the gallows pole, prisoners saw lively swallows darting over Italian hills arrayed with vineyards and poplar trees. If hope is this delusion, I have no use for it. But I believe hope is not a gallows screen. Hope is what keeps us climbing the stairs toward gallows we know full well await us, which is what we do so nobly and what has become our art, our beauty, our cause for celebration.

To carry on, to continue, to make or find what gentle beauty we can before our lives end—this is the thing with feathers even when its head falls off.

My friend Franz died in September, torn apart by a collision with a fuel truck. Here is how I remember him, eighteen hours before he died. Sitting in a camp chair in front of a U.S. Forest Service sign that read, "Do Not Feed the Animals," he was feeding the birds, breaking bread into small pieces and tucking the pieces into his wool cap, into folds on his shoulders, putting pieces of bread on his knees, in the crook of his elbow, holding bread out in his hand. A gray jay landed with a hop on his head and pecked the bread. Standing right there on the tassel of Franz's hat, the jay craned its head and looked around for more.

A jay landed on his knee. Another swooped across his face to take the offering from his shoulder. Jays gathered in the branches above him and dropped onto his head. With his eyes scrunched shut and his smile beatific, my friend was hidden behind a flurry of gray feathers, flaring tails, the swirling, crying birds. This did not keep him from dying, but for that moment, it seemed as if he could fly.

Morning in Romero Canyon

At first, the morning is flat as a sketch—sleeping bag laid out on a stone slab, narrow creek flowing from left to right, hillside filling most of the page. What texture there is seems to be drawn in lead pencil. Sound is flat and monochrome, too, the creek seeping steadily rock to rock. People call it white noise, but today it's pale gray.

I boil creek water, pour a cup of tea, and sit cross-legged on sand, looking west. I know the sun will rise at my back. Under the weight of desert light, shadow will slowly sink down the mountainside in front of me. I hope it hurries. The morning is very, very cold.

I can figure out how long it will take for the sun to *set* at this latitude. When my hand is at arm's length, pointing sideways, the width of each of my fingers is fifteen minutes to sunset. The sun must also take just this long to *rise*, given the regularity of things. I lift my hand in front of the hill. Three fingers: forty-five minutes before light will travel from the crest to the bottomland where I sit. I tuck my hands into my armpits, wishing I had re-membered to bring gloves.

There's already a little bit of light tangled in the top of an ancient cottonwood tree upstream. Light had no sooner hit the tree than birds began to sing; I think I could close my eyes and track the sun by birdsong. I could close my eyes and track the time of day by the song of the creek too. It's so cold at night that the snowfields at the head of the canyon freeze up and the flow of water slows and drops to a single tone, a cello maybe. When sun strikes the snowfields, the creek will become all flutes and bells, fortissimo. I close my eyes and listen: yellow-rumped warblers, the thrumming creek, and the cooing mourning dove, an overture so dependable you could set your watch by that soft sound, an hour before dawn.

"There is something infinitely healing in the repeated refrains of nature," Rachel Carson wrote. "The assurance that dawn comes after night, and spring after winter." I have never felt this so strongly as I do now, waiting for the sun to warm my back. The bottom may drop out of my life, what I trusted may fall away completely, leaving me astonished and shaken. But still, sticky leaves emerge from bud scales that curl off the tree as the sun crosses the sky. Darkness pools and drains away, and the curve of the new moon points to the place the sun will rise again. There is wild comfort in the cycles and the intersecting circles, the rotations and revolutions, the growing and ebbing of this beautiful and strangely trustworthy world.

I settle back on the rock and drag my sleeping bag over my knees. Diffuse light silvers the water; I can just make out a dragonfly nymph that crawls toward the surface with no expectation of flight beyond maybe a tightness in the carapace across its back. No matter how hard it tries or doesn't, there will come a time when the dragonfly pumps the crinkles out of its wings, and there they will be, luminous as mica, threaded with lapis and gold.

No measure of human grief can stop Earth in its tracks. Earth rolls into sunlight and rolls away again, continents glowing green and gold under the clouds. Trust this, and there will come a time when dogged, desperate trust in the world will break open into wonder. Wonder leads to gratitude. Gratitude opens onto peace.

When I look up from the creek, the boulders on top of the hill are yellow, as if highway crews had painted them in passing. Here's the tall stalk of a century plant, tan against blue sky. Now an ocotillo flower blazes red. Slowly, slowly, a rock distinguishes itself from the hill, yellow with a sharp shadow that falls on a brittlebush that itself suddenly bursts into yellow bloom, first the top of the bush, then the whole glorious thing.

Birds grow restless in the sudden light that floods into the crevice below the stone. A canyon wren bursts into song. Its falling notes tumble from rock to rock the way light seems to fall: not in any hurry. Such gifts cannot be rushed, this light shawling down the hill, this descending song. Desert morning comes if you notice it or not, whether or not you are asleep, say, or if your eyes are closed, crying. But when you look up, there it is. The spatulas of the prickly pear catch the sun full in the face. Each crack in the rock is revealed, each bare stem and each stem's shadow. A viceroy butterfly opens its wings, flaps them experimentally, starts up for the day. Then it flies across the ravines and hummocks of the hill. Its shadow slides up to meet it, then dips away.

Light has reached the edge of the creek, each pebble rippled. As the water pools and drops, so the light swirls and tumbles down river. I could imagine that it is melted morning that fills this sculptured bed, throwing light onto the underside of rocks, rippling light on the yellow devil's fiddles. The leaves of overhanging cottonwoods flitter with light. The creek flitters too, the sound livelier now, like a sparrow. Suddenly I see frogs. I had thought there were pebbles embedded in the midstream sandstone boulders, but they are frogs sticking to the rock. I've heard of these canyon tree frogs, but I don't know if I've ever noticed them before. What does sun feel like to skin that has been buried all winter, waiting stolidly for spring?

And here it is, the sun's warmth on my back.

In full light now, I take off my wool hat to let the sun warm my head. I don't look at the sun, but I know it's there. I can feel it with the back of my neck. I can see it in the shadow that stretches in front of me.

The Patience of Herons

At dusk in Alaska, I went onto the cabin porch to check on the herons. Frank and I had been watching them off and on since we came back from fishing, propping binoculars on the porch rail. There'd been four birds in the cove, but with rain driving in and night coming on, only one was left. Rain beaded on its back and dripped off the point of its beak. Before the squall, the heron had balanced on the perfect reflection of one gray leg. But in this downpour, its legs poked into water as opaque as a shattered windshield. The heron shrugged its shoulders, then slowly unfurled its wings and held them at full length. Under that umbrella, the wing-shaped patches of water became smooth and still.

What could the heron see then? Speckled gravel, surely. That's what I see when I wade in the cove at low tide. Sea lettuce, broken mussels, a pyramid of silt around a sand shrimp's hole. But probably not a tiny flounder or stickleback, because the heron stood without moving, frozen in exactly that position, barely breathing as far as I could see.

What goes through a heron's head, standing that still? The ache between its shoulders? The tug of tide against its knees? Is it dreaming of blennies or cursing the cramp in its leg? I don't know, but I have seen the way freshwater flows over saltwater and, where the current folds one into the other, the way the moving water turns visible itself, and gelid, and objects seen through it are like dreams, waving and indistinct, as if all the water had gone to old glass. The heron's mind may be like that, so clear that the clarity becomes a thing in itself, and when a small flounder floats into view, it's like a silver coin caught in ice.

On the porch, water dripped from the raincoats we had hung under the eaves to dry, rain poured from the porch roof onto thimbleberry leaves, pounded the cove. But the heron held on. Wings lifted, neck outstretched, eyes on the water, the heron waited.

Herons aren't born knowing patience. They have to learn, and this process was painful to watch. When the young ones showed up in the cove a few weeks ago, their own mothers and fathers ignored them and went about their business, even though the young ones teetered on the gravel bar, seeming to be afraid of the water. All day they stood there, watching their parents gag down fish. By the time I came out on the porch on the second tide, the young ones were in the water, darting their necks around but unwilling, I thought, to get their heads wet.

The third tide was stormy. The spruce on the island flailed in the wind and an eagle, when it tried to land in the spruce's spire, tumbled and grabbed at the branches. On that briny, spicy morning, the young herons chased wildly through the shallows, high-stepping with their backward knees, tipping, flailing, jabbing at the water—all for nothing.

On the fourth tide, they were standing in the cove as still as their parents, starved into stillness, maybe exhausted into stillness. The tide flowed past their rusty knees, past the hard alertness of their eyes. I imagine that's when a flounder lifted off the sand, betrayed by a puff of silt. And so the herons learned patience, which may be a lesson in trust: Trust that the tide will move its slow steady way from the cove, and then it will seep in again. You can't see it come or go, but it comes and goes. You have to trust in this. Eventually, surely, the sea lettuce will float and a sculpin will reveal itself, diving for cover. Sustenance will come with time, the way the tide comes with time. Open your wings and wait.

"Patience" comes from the same ancient roots as "petals"—to open like a flower, to unfurl, to receive the stroke of a moth's tongue and the ministrations of a bee. And so we are given "passive" and "patient" and "passionate." The philosopher Spinoza thought that passion was the opposite of action: to be acted upon rather than to act. And so a heron is passionate in this odd, old-fashioned way—open, unresisting, transparent, suffering the sense impressions to flow through its mind, exquisitely aware, a single still point of clarity.

"Watch now," Frank said suddenly. I lifted my binoculars, wondering what he had noticed. The heron took a slow step forward, barely disturbing the water. That motion brought its body under its neck, coiling its neck like a spring. A splash as the head hit the water. Then the heron flipped its beak toward the sky and swallowed a silver flash.

I knew immediately that I had underestimated patience. A heron's mind may be open to the flow of events, but it's open the way a leghold trap is open. Taut and dangerous, precisely balanced, holding, this patience is so intense that it's ready, at one ruffled shadow, to release its spring and stab. The trap sprang so fast that I never saw the end of the heron's terrible attentiveness, that snap. I saw the splash of beak into water. But the point of release was so singular, so utterly all-or-nothing, yes or no, that

I would not have been surprised to have heard a metallic click. There is nothing flaccid in a heron's patience.

"I need to know what it feels like to be stabbed by a heron," I told Frank, and was surprised to hear myself say it.

"Well, we could try the experiment with a knife," Frank said, surprised himself. "Herons drive their beaks through the skin of a halibut. How many of our knives are sharp enough to do that?" Right. Once he mentioned it, I remembered watching a heron drag a flounder onto the beach and stab it to death with one blow.

The heron was still standing in the cove when it got too dark to see. Before we went into the cabin for bed, we looked back once more. We could make out the silhouette of the eagle in the top of the spruce, its back hunched against the sky.

I know a man who saw an eagle kill a heron. He was watching a heron hunt in the trout creek that borders his ranch. It was raining off and on, light winds. The heron was having some slow success with small brook trout that swam in the shadows. It had just lifted its head and swallowed a trout, when a bald eagle swooped down, wings broad as a blanket, and covered the heron, pressing it to the stones. Then the eagle hunched its shoulders, bent down its razor beak, and slit the length of the heron's neck. It seized the trout that spilled from the wound, and flapped into the trees, yelling wildly. The body of the heron, its neck extended and long legs trailing, rotated slowly down the creek.

I think I have heard, although I didn't see, a bobcat take a heron. We were camped on a gravel bar next to the Alsea River in Oregon. It was drizzling, so the tent was closed up and noisy itself, but there was no missing this sequence of sounds. A snarl, a wild scream from a heron, the sound of splashing and tearing feathers, then nothing. Frank and I questioned each other half the night. What else could that have been? In the morning, there were bobcat tracks in the mud across the river, but no sign of a bird, not a pinfeather.

So I don't know what to think about people who tell their grieving friends to be patient. "Be patient. Time is the great healer. Give it time." Have these people ever watched a heron hunt, ever heard one die in the dark? What are they thinking? There are many kinds of patience, and maybe they work against each other. Patience is active *and* passive. I would call patience a paradox, except that's too simple.

Here is the work of patience: to die to the world of acting, the world of hoping, and so to open oneself to the suffering of the whole world. This is true passion, taking in the suffering of all together. This patience is the birth of compassion.

And here is the work of patience: to become brave and fierce, set like a spring to seize whatever life puts in the way of our stiletto beaks. To stalk it and impale it and with a flip of our muscular necks, to fling it into the air and swallow it whole. Seize the day in a razor beak. This patience is the birth of joy.

And here is the work of patience: to be ready for the world to slit us, the full length of us, opening our hearts with the pellucid attention that is the watchfulness of the heron in the cove at the end of the day, when wood smoke slides onto the rising tide and slanting rain pocks the water. This patience is the birth of gratitude.

I don't know. It's easy to be wrong about birds. My experience is that as soon as I write down the moral of a story about the natural world, something takes me by surprise. So I wasn't exactly surprised when my son called to say that he had been hiking down by the river, a gravel beach, cloudy day. He almost stumbled over the body of a great blue heron. Its neck was stretched out and its beak was agape, and stuck half in its throat, half out, was the corpse of the biggest bullfrog my son had ever seen.

The Water and the Wave

Frank crouches over the helm, staring through a crescent cleared by a single, stuttering windshield wiper. He cranks the wheel to starboard, to port, zigzagging in the confused sea to meet each wave head-on. The bow dives into a trough, rears up, and slams down again, raising a wall of spray. "We're getting slapped around," Frank shouts in his calmest voice, "but nothing the boat can't handle."

Maybe he is right and maybe he is wrong. I look again at the GPS. We are trying to cross the windward reach of Icy Strait, a trough that channels wind and currents from the Gulf of Alaska. Here, Icy Strait hurtles into Chatham Strait, a long fetch that rides up the Northwest Pacific Coast. Tides rip through from three directions, and no wonder the sea is what Frank calls "messy" and I call terrifying.

When our friends' son died last winter—a terrible loss of a strong young man—his father asked if I would write the memorial service. Yes, I will, I said, but what I thought was, my heart is breaking for this man who has picked up the phone and dialed the numbers to make plans for the future. How can that be possible? What I thought was, I hope they understand that I don't know how to do what they ask. But then, they don't know how to go on—who could?

"You should talk to someone who has done a memorial service before," Frank said, and that seemed right. So the next morning, I was sitting in the office of the Unitarian minister, leaning over a cup of her tea. Never before had I wished so desperately to be part of a church. Then I could take a book off the shelf, open it to the right page, and read the powerful ancient words. *Surely goodness and mercy shall follow me all the days of my life.* Then this death would be Death, and this sorrow would be Sorrow, and none of us would be so terribly alone, so pitiably inventive, like little children who climb onto the kitchen counter to make dinner when their parents don't come home.

"Make a vessel," the minister was saying. "Make a vessel big enough to hold everyone and their grief. Hold them, carry them, in this vessel." She raised her open hands to outline the shape. A dory, I thought, red cedar, rockered fore and aft. "Find those words," she said.

I have to look at the GPS to find us because there's no telling where we are from the view out the sides of this boat. Clouds obscure the mountains and fog rides the back of the waves, so all I can make out is the presence or absence of a darker smudge along the horizon, which may be Point Adolphus or the mainland or an expanse of sea without landfall until the Aleutian Islands, straight west.

Waves rise and give way randomly, skinned every shade of gray, teethed white. There is no way forward through this chaos. But in our wake, the path we have taken trails out behind us like a country lane, smooth and green between wakes that peel off to port and starboard. The fact of going forward creates a path. I don't understand why, but it seems to be so.

I want to call out to Frank, "Turn the boat around. The path is behind us." But this would worry him, this insanity. He has to count on me. I help watch the GPS, the charts, the route, warning of shoals or kelp beds, floating logs or whales. It will not do for me to be backward-looking or unaware, or to allow a collision with a whale basking at the surface with only its dorsal fin exposed, black as the turn of any one of a thousand waves.

A vessel. The minister surprised me. I thought she would give me an order of service or something equally solid. Instead, she gave me a metaphor.

There was silence between us as I tried to imagine a vessel with this broad a beam and strong a hull. But all I could envision was my own son, alone in a rowboat at dawn, rowing out from the cove to an eelgrass bed beginning to sway under a falling tide. Mist rose around him, so he rowed into and out of invisibility as the eelgrass bent and dipped under the lick of dawn water. Many are the ways we probe the forms that the real world takes, the things we do not understand. So strong or weak is our faith in the boats we build and the strength of the sea to hold us.

A comber catches our bow and throws it sideways. With one hand, Frank cranks us back into the waves and with the other, yanks back on the throttle. We are crawling up and down these waves as they heave under us. How will we ever make headway? I try to calm myself, to breathe with the up and down, but my breath comes in gasps and cries. I fix my eyes on the bulk of a headland that is slowly emerging ten degrees to port, willing it to come closer, willing us to carom finally into its lee.

So gradually that I don't see it happen, the waves smooth to hills and we slide from the fog bank into the world. I look at Frank. He wipes the salt spray off his glasses and avoids meeting my eyes. And now the sea is rippled glass, blue blackened with cloud shadows. On the island peaks, the sun roams over alpine meadows. A league ahead, a whale exhales. Slowly, the black back curves into the air, rolls underwater, and the spreading tail lifts like a black tulip rising toward morning.

> Where is the boat big enough to carry all this grief, to lift us on the strength of the water and let us float there in a safe place, days and long nights, as the sun sets in a strip of saffron, as the moon rises through fog the long cold nights?
>
> There are waves—the chaotic movement of time and substance, change through time, the living and the dying, the striving and the giving up, the struggle for meaning and safety, this beauty and danger. There is water—the form of this, the transparent substance, the fact of lifting, that grace. Waves can dash us down. But water will hold us up.

Frank brings us close to land and cuts the engine to study the charts. It's shoaly water here where our route rounds the reef at

Point Retreat. Fronds of kelp curl in small currents, lifting on the swell. Sunlight slides down the mountain and lights the rock wrack, a yellow rim between the forest and the sea. In the quiet of our relief, we can hear the ocean breathe and sneeze, the sigh of a kelp bed coming to rest on its side, the squeak of rubbery stems settling on mussel beds. Barnacles click and anemones shrug shut as water draws away from the land into a bulge that slides around the Earth—all the water in the seas lifting toward the moon, slipping away from bays and mudflats and sea lettuce rocks, lifting toward what is so far away that all we know of it is light, and even this washes out in the glare of the sun.

"It's a good boat, that handled those seas," I say to Frank.

Two ravens sail from the headland and cut over the boat, so close I can hear the slice of their wings.

> Where would I find the red cedar planks and alder staves that would make this brave boat?

> Friends had sent poems. It's a remarkable thing that most people go through life with barely a nod to a poem, but when death comes, only poetry is enough. Maybe that's because poems say exactly what is grow-ing inchoate in our minds, the way snowflakes form from fog and fall in beautiful, sharp-edged patterns on our gloves. Or maybe poems calm us with their perfection—nothing more to say—the way a hand on our forehead silenced us as children and satisfied us. Enough, a mother says. That's enough.

> They sent Mozart, which seemed just right to me. Music is the closest thing I know to water, where there is no thought, only purity of sensation, a kind of immersion, to be drawn into the currents of sound, to be moved the way that water moves the light.

They sent memories, the stories, the strength of them. Memories are real. Sharp edged, deep grained, long fibered, solid—they can't be checked by death. We can float in the reality of memory. The autumn color of his hair, the flash of his smile, solid in the minds of people who love him—these are the black-locust ribs, shaped by the spokeshave, sanded smooth. People say he lives on in memory, but that's not quite right. The memories live on, and they are full of life. Nothing can take them from us. What I mean is that a life that was beautiful and well-lived was in fact beautiful and well-lived, even if it came to an end long before its time.

Each memory put him in a place—running with his cousins on the beach or finning in shafts of underwater light, parting the kelp stems with his hands while small fish shimmered away. Those places hold the shape of his passing through; the patterns of silver fish, the sway of kelp, the sift of sand are the Earth's memories of a boy.

When we finally reach the safety of our cove, so close to home that we can see afternoon light reflecting off the windows of our cabin, the tide is out, and the expanse of exposed tideland blocks our way to the mooring. We will have to wait for the tide to rise and carry us home.

Frank noses the boat into the gravel and lifts the engine. We sit in the stern in the sun and wait, knowing that the water will return and float us into the cove. We can see it coming over the clam beds, the shine rising between gray pebbles. Scraps of popweed float past, and sometimes an opalescent mussel shell, floating like a dory. Water rises under us. The skiff lurches, the aluminum bow still caught on cobbles, and the stern swings around. Slowly, we bump into the cove backward, leaning over the gunwales to watch through the water. The little channel is lined with blue mussels and barnacles coated with pink algae. A Dungeness crab folds in its angles and wedges between stones.

Now the stern hangs up on a rock and the bow swings around, slinging us past a bed of spiny sea urchins and sea wrack hanging by its holdfasts to the cobbles. Then it swings us into the path of the sun, and all we see is light. We wait there, warmed, until the tide turns us again. Gulls shake out their feathers and settle onto the sand. A crab carapace floats past, chips of shining mica, a spruce cone reduced by a squirrel to a cob. We don't float alone. The whole world glides along. Tide lifts the stern off the rock. We float quickly now, almost home, eddying over deeper water and a sandy bottom. Young flounder flee in front of us, so perfectly matched to the sand that a puff of dust and a riffle in the water are the only signs they have gone.

"How can it be, this sudden end?" I asked Frank.

"How can it be," he asked in return, "that life?"

These are mysteries that have no answer. Do we have any choice but to wait for time and tide to ferry us, grieving and bewildered, to a place of peace? In that slow time, we can take comfort in what we know—that all of us come from the ocean, its water and light. That someday each of us will be folded back into the waves. And that this process of coming to life is beautiful and important and radiant with love.

The boat floats broadside into flooding beach grass and lodges there, rocking gently. Our haul-out rope floats alongside us, gathering seaweed. With a boat hook, Frank lifts the rope off the water and pulls us in, hand over hand. We come to shore by the mouth of the creek that enters the cove through alder trees and huckleberries. Where tidewater nudges into freshwater, young salmon, striped like rippling sun, vanish into the light of the mingled waters.

Stillwater Bay, Columbia River

To see to the depth of a river, wade into still water. In the silent space under the slick of the world, the river clears. If you stand still too, so as not to wrinkle the water, you will see the shadows of minnows. You will smell sage and melting snow and you will notice, incised into the topography of the silt, little river channels pointing to the sea. And isn't this what you had hoped to find? A quiet place where everything comes clear and the Earth itself shows the way to the one thing.

To Mend a Broken Pot

At the low river levels this early in spring, the current moves
about three miles an hour. It's a perfect pace for a canoe. We
slip through shadows cast by the high cliffs of the Green River's
Labyrinth Canyon. The river rounds a tight curve and our canoe is back in the sun, floating past sandbars choked with salt
cedar and willow. Birds come alive in the sun. We hear the rock
wren's *tick-ear tick-ear* and the catcall of the spotted towhee. The
mud nests of cliff swallows line up in cracks in the canyon walls.
Last summer, each would have been a perfect little clay jar with
a narrow-necked opening, but by now their tops have been broken off by winter. Winter has done its work on the high canyon
walls too. They look like they're kneeling on the broken slabs of
their faces. Frank points out an arched vault in the rock face and
below it, a slab with exactly the same arch. What a thunder that
would have made, falling. We stop paddling to listen to the song
of the canyon wren, a sweet descending scale.

The green river reflects the polished red walls and impossibly blue sky. If anything grows old gracefully, it is a desert river canyon. This is a grace I would aspire to. It's an open question—how to make something beautiful of the pieces that are left after time does the slow work of the river, giving and taking, taking away.

We camp that night on a sandbar at the mouth of a side canyon. I go out after firewood while Frank rigs a pole to hang the teakettle over the fire. Looking for sticks carried by spring storms, I climb up a streambed that tumbles over sand and rock between two cliffs. There is ice in the north-facing coves and green pools of water in white sand. Where the canyon heads in an amphitheater of towering rock, I come across broken sherds of pottery, painted black with white lines. The sherds are scattered over the ledge as if they had been swept down from the cliffs above, and maybe they had been.

It might be wrong to disturb them, but isn't it a basic human impulse to try to fit pieces together? And this is what I do, gathering a small pile of sherds with the same white decoration, lining them up this way and that. But I fail to make anything whole, and I put the sherds back as well as I can in the places I found them. We eat that night in the smoke of a juniper fire, knowing that other people have built juniper fires beside this rock, have lived and grown beside this rock, have seen their lives fragment and fall, growing old among these ancient rocks.

I wake up to a desert chill that smells of dust and willows. The rock wrens are chirring, although it's still dark. Just as the sun outlines the skyline in gold, the canyon wrens begin to sing. When they stop to listen for an answering scale, the canyon is utterly silent. A rock thuds, echoing across the river, then the silence again. Never have I heard such complete quiet.

Frank stirs, then unzips his sleeping bag. Before long, I smell a juniper fire. I sit up and dress myself in my pillow—the fleece shirt I used as a pillowcase, the down vest that served as stuffing. I've been thinking all night about the broken pottery on the canyon ledge, remembering what Christopher has told me about what to do with broken pieces. Chris is my son-in-law, a conservator of ceramics at the Arizona State Museum. His job is to keep objects from falling apart, or if they have already fallen apart, to figure how to put the pieces back together again.

"To mend a clay pot," Chris told me, "the Hohokam people sometimes drilled holes along the broken edges and sewed the pieces together."

He held one hand at chest height, putting downward pressure on an imaginary piece of wood notched to fit the top end of a drill. The other hand shuttled back and forth as if it were playing an invisible cello. That's the hand that moves the bow, a curved piece of alder wood strung with sinew. The sinew is wrapped once around the drill; as the hand moves back and forth, the bow-drill spins against the cracked pottery.

Chris's hands are white, with long fingers and slow movements. He did this imagined work carefully, stopping to adjust an invisible pot in his lap, ensuring that the drill would make a hole in exactly the right place. He thought it would have taken most of a day for someone to drill the holes, squinting in the spotty shade under an ocotillo ramada.

"It's probably a woman who fixed this pot," he had said when I asked, "because it's the women who shape the clay." And this made sense to my imagination, the dogged fixing—a woman determined to keep things together, now that her mother has passed on and her sons are grown—her frustration with the jasper drill tip that skids off the slope of the jar. Once the holes are drilled, she walks into the desert to cut spears of yucca. She pounds them between stones until she can pull the fibers loose.

Rolling the fibers together, rubbing palm against thigh, she makes cord. This would feel good, the pressure against stiff muscles. She threads the fiber through the holes she has drilled, aligning the cracks, pulling the ends of the cord tightly together to bind up the pot. Then she ties off the knot.

Chris's hands moved up and down, sewing. Then he reached out his long arms and cupped his hands, as if he cradled a pot. "Good as new," he announced, and it seemed to please him, his imagined repair.

Chris couldn't tell how his imagined pot broke. Had she fallen, carrying it up from the fields? A life is full of these chances. Was she an old woman when it fell from her hands? There are accidents, I know. *Things fall apart.* That's what accident means: in Latin, *accidere*, to fall on, to fall down. Sometimes it's only the weight of time that breaks the curve of a jar—the crushing accumulation of dust and sliding rock and dried leaves falling.

She would have valued the pot very highly to have taken this time to weave its broken edges back together, Chris said. She could have used pine pitch as glue to mend the pot if she hadn't cared about having a strong seam. And not only pitch; the people make glues from plant gums and tree resins and animal hides boiled to jelly. There is a pot in the collection, Chris said, that was mended with glue made of pelican fat mixed with the lacquer exuded from the back end of a beetle that lives on the creosote bush.

This delighted me. People say it's good to have a lawyer in every family, or an accountant, but I am glad for this fixer. I would apprentice myself to his craft and follow him around, boiling up glue and sticking things back together again.

Chris led me into the museum. The Arizona State Museum has a floor-to-ceiling glass case that curves through the hall, displaying two hundred pottery bowls and jars: a thousand-year-old pitcher whose slouching shape gives away a pitcher's ancestry as a gourd and whose corrugations give away its origin in coils of clay; a white Zia jar, painted with a rooster; a seed jar with a tiny pouting mouth.

I leaned close to the glass to study a large clay jar made by a Hohokam artisan who worked the clay of the Gila River a thousand years ago. Someone had reassembled it from at least a hundred sherds, the largest no bigger than my hand. They were glued together like puzzle pieces. But many of the pieces were missing, leaving voids that opened onto the shadows inside. Even so, I could make out the pattern of gray lizards swimming through swirls that might have been disturbances on the surface of a desert tiñaja or waves laid down in sandstone. Lacing the jar were the threads of shadowed cracks between the pieces. If I hadn't known the cracks were breaks in the clay, I might have thought they were the net that held the pot together.

Frank and I see the same gray lizards in the canyon we hike after breakfast. A faint trail climbs a rock-choked wash between junipers undercut by floods. On one side of the trail, the dry riverbed falls over boulders. That's where we see the lizards, peering out of a crack in the wall, letting the sun warm the wedges of their heads. Frank and I climb quietly this morning, placing our feet deliberately. The prickly pears are thin as cardboard. When we climb around a turn in the canyon wall, a crow lifts off, dragging its shadow through the scrub. I am glad for the chance to pause; the canyon is rocky and steep. I rub my fingers through hopsage leaves and bring them to my nose. These are the things I see and touch, but I am thinking about moments that have passed.

We started hiking desert canyons with our children when our son was too short to climb the slick-rock dry falls. I would lean my back against the rock and let him clamber up my body as if I were a ladder—bracing on my knees, my hips, climbing off my shoulders in jogging shoes that closed with Velcro flaps. Along the trail, he turned every flat rock, hoping for scorpions, and stirred the brush with sticks. He wore a desert hat shading his face. Our daughter picked yarrow leaves and rubbed them in her hair. She dove after lizards, cupping her hands over the place they had been and then lifting one hand to find they had gone. Brother and sister, they lay on their backs on the rocks, contorting their arms and legs, hanging out their tongues, trying to draw in vultures for a closer look.

With their little sleeping bags between our larger ones, we slept out on rock ledges scattered with pottery sherds and fishhook cactus. I would wake early with my children and husband beside me—the first warming light, the first calls of the mourning doves, the sharp smell of desert dust and juniper, drinking it in, the way we were together, and I would find that my children were awake too, lying rigid with excitement in their sleeping bags, gulping the liquid anticipation of that day.

Then one year, the kids climbed steeply, farther than they had ever climbed before, up the bed of a dry fall, wedging between shining boulders. When we came to a sharp overhang where the trail threaded the edge of a cliff, Frank and I decided to wait. We leaned back against warm rock and watched our children scramble up the trail, appearing and disappearing, until they emerged in the distance, waving their arms from a bulge of rimrock across the gulch.

This morning, when Frank and I come to a steep pitch, I look back reflexively, a mother making sure her children are following. There are no children, of course, although there are vultures. Many things are missing from the trail this morning: our children gone to their own lives in distant cities, the youth and bandy strength of my legs, a future that once seemed to have no end. What I want to know is how to take the parts that remain, the empty spaces, even the cracks, and fit them into something whole and meaningful, shaped with the kind of care that would cause a woman to spend all day drilling and stitching, drilling and stitching, trying to make strong thread by rubbing her palms against her sore thighs.

"Can't you fix this?" I had asked Chris. "Couldn't you mend these cracks so perfectly that no one could tell the jar had been broken?"

"I could," he said, looking up, surprised maybe at the urgency in my voice. "I would find a potsherd from the same period of time, from the same clay bank, of a perfectly matching color. I would grind it fine and mix it with glue. With a paint brush made of a single sable hair, I would paint this into the finest cracks. When I was done, no one would know that the pot had ever been broken."

His hands went to work again, testing the consistency of imagined clay sand by rubbing his thumb across his fingertips. His long, thin back bent over the work. Then he raised his head and grinned.

"But I would never do that."

I protested. "Even when you could make it whole again?"

"It's wrong," he said, "to take away the story a pot can tell."

A pot should tell about the passing of time. It should speak of the woman with swirls on her fingertips, who smoothed the inside surface with a piece of gourd. It should raise a prickle of wonder at the artist who looked at a lizard and saw the geometry of its back limbs, right angles framing the curve of its tail. It should lay bare the disaster of its breaking and what else might have been broken with it. If it has empty spaces in its skin, that emptiness is part of what it is.

Clay that holds a story of human creative power holds also a story of the fragmenting power of time and weather and irretrievable loss. The beauty in a bowl is the truth of it. If part of its truth is the wounds it has endured, then those wounds are part of its beauty.

"Here's what I mean," Chris said, and he pointed through the glass of the display case. I leaned forward to see the jar he was pointing to, but in the reflection on the glass, all I could see was the face of a woman. She might have been an old woman; I couldn't tell. Her hair was wilder than I remembered mine to be. Lines creased her upper lip, and above her lifted eyebrows, her forehead was corrugated in wrinkles.

Frank thinks that the sound I took to be a falling rock this morning was in fact a beaver thudding its tail on the water. So I take off my shoes and set out from camp to look for tracks. The silt that rims the island is so fine that I sink to my ankles and stumble to keep from sliding into the river. Geese have certainly visited the island while we were up the canyon. And around the foot of the island are unmistakable signs of beavers. Their bare feet sink in the mud too, leaving perfect imprints of paws and dragged sticks. But here I stop and pull out binoculars.

Swallows alight on a patch of mud next to the water. They poke their beaks into the mud, then roll it and work it into a perfect ball. A swallow flies away with a mud ball in its mouth, lands on the circular remnant of last year's nest, jabs the new mud ball into position on the broken wall, and then swoops back for another mouthful of mud. All the broken nests tucked into the cliff have a row of shiny wet mud balls around their circumferences. At this rate, there will be a whole neighborhood of little stuck-together clay jugs on the cliff by nightfall.

I scoop up a handful of swallow mud and wade back to camp. I choose a flat rock and sit down to work. To do this right, I would work the mud in my mouth, mixing silt and saliva into a sticky ball. I decide against this. Instead, I pry out a small piece of mud, spit on it, roll it round between my hands, and press it onto the stone. And then another and another, while the shadows thrown by an old oak shorten and the wrens fall silent. It's a squat, cock-eyed swallow's nest that I finally manage to make. Even though the sides are not hard to stack, rounding the curve toward the opening, my nest sags and threatens to collapse, and I give up on making a spout. But the velvet sand has its own beauty and an honorable history, sifted from magnificent cliffs by time and the river. I prop it up with twigs as well as I can and set it in the sun to dry.

Repeat the Sounding Joy

While fields and floods, rocks, hills, and plains
Repeat the sounding joy,
Repeat the sounding joy,
Repeat, repeat the sounding joy.
— ISAAC WATTS

Fields

WREN, OREGON

In spring's low afternoon light, the field was a place of silence and secrets. Swallows swept over the pond, but if they lisped the way they sometimes do, I did not hear them. The crows perched in the old oak seemed stunned into silence by the unexpected sun. Even the colors seemed subdued, new grass still hidden under last winter's silver weeds. When I walked through the field to my writer's cabin, I was embarrassed by the noise my jeans made, scratching against dry stalks of tarweed and thistle. I stopped short when I thought I heard a garter snake sliding through the grasses, but I might have heard a seed spinning down or a beetle spreading its wings—the field was that quiet. At the desk in my cabin, I wrote in a silence broken only by a fly at the window. When a red-tailed hawk screamed, I jumped and hit my knees against the desk.

As the afternoon went on, the field turned its shoulder to the sun and the light came in low and cold. I got up and walked down to the pond. Geese that had been sleeping on the floating log stood up, shook their backsides, and honked. They honked without ceasing, rousing the crows that began to yell. Steller's jays, which had been quiet until now, swooped through the oaks, clattering. My neighbor started up a chainsaw.

A yellow streak outlined the hills. I spread my sleeping bag in the cabin and tucked myself in. Blue clouds overwhelmed the sunset, and the first frog called. I know this was a tree frog no bigger than my thumb, but its sound was huge. *Crack-crick, crack-crick*, and I wondered at its courage, the first frog to sing. Somehow this encouraged the others, and instantly the whole valley was filled with frog calls. This was not a thin thread of song or a Bach chorale. This was a thousand falsetto soloists backed by a heavy metal band trying to get the rhythm right. This was grindcore. This was open mike at the mosh pit, the riffs and shout-outs, and drummers completely out of synch. The dogs started up barking and the geese joined in. Full night fell as the frogs and dogs hollered whoopee.

But it was a sudden silence that woke me up.

The night was very dark.

What had quieted the frogs? A raccoon? A coyote? A human intruder? I lay still, listening, the way prey listen. There was a rumble from the west. A frog called once and hushed itself. Another rumble and a flash of light. Wind rattled the roof. Then light strobed and instantly, a rumble grew big and cracked apart. Silence then. Waiting. A single frog ventured to call. Another answered. Then the full chorus rose from the pond. The storm blew in—first the wind, then the lashing rain. I lay safe and warm in my sleeping bag while rain shouldered into the side of the cabin, lightning flashed, thunder rolled over the hills, dogs barked. And the frogs? Frogs sang and sang, joy to the world, the rain and the lightning. Joy to the world, the thunder and the night.

Floods

ARTIC, WASHINGTON

We knew from the radio that the "storm of the century" had hit the Washington coast, raising Grays River and the East Fork so high that the rivers joined in one swirling pool, knocking down the alders and rainforest. That's where Frank's brother lives, in a trailer court beside Big Creek. Worried, we drove up as soon as we heard that state troopers had reopened the road. Even three days after the flood, we had to dodge rock slides and downed trees and swerve around orange cones that marked undercut macadam. It was raining hard. The yellow lights of highway crews smeared in each swipe of our windshield wipers. Just past the Artic Tavern, we turned down the road where John lives. This is no paved parking lot. This is the wild Pacific edge, a few silver trailers tucked under immense, moss-darkened Douglas-fir, back in the huckleberries and ferns.

In the aftermath of the storm, the trailer park looked like a log deck, half-buried under fallen trees so big that I couldn't see over their trunks. People had already taken chainsaws to some of the shattered cedars, reducing them to broad stumps, piles of yellow sawdust, and neat ricks of cordwood. Mud, thrown up by root wads torn from the dirt by the weight of falling trees, still splattered the trailers. John was one of the men working a saw, a tall square-faced man with a silver braid down his back.

We walked together to the tavern, wading through puddles and windrows of flood debris. The stories started even before the girl at the bar could draw the beers.

"We all holed up in the tavern when the storm came," John said. "I mean, it was taking your life in your hands to go outside. All that rain loosened up the roots, and when the wind blew in, those trees just went over, one tree taking down the next. We could hear them go. It'd be spooky quiet, then we could hear the wind starting to come, just this whisper, then, man, it was like a freight train was headed right for us, everything shaking and the candle flames blowing straight to the side, and then *crack*, a tree let loose, snapping its roots and crashing down. We could feel it through the floor, and we'd listen real close to see if the sound was cracking wood or splitting aluminum, and whose place was going next."

John scooted his chair over to make room for another friend and kept talking. There must have been five of them at the table by now, gray-haired men, easy in their chairs.

"My buddy says, man, you gotta help me. I gotta get my truck out before it gets smashed. So I got my peavey and my chainsaw and we went out in that weather. Dark? Whoa. It was crazy— no wind, just this smell of cedar trees so thick you could drink it—and then we got slammed with wind so strong my buddy grabs me and we're running along with the wind, trying not to. Wind smacked us into the side of a pickup, couldn't help it. The river had crossed the highway and ran down the road into the trailer park, pushing all this stuff. Limbs and electric wires. Trees are down everywhere. My buddy has a flashlight, but we can't tell what's ground and what's flood, everything covered in blowdown—ferns and moss and limbs and siding. We'd hear a tree crack and we'd tuck our heads down into our necks, like that's going to keep a limb from pile-driving us."

Somebody at the bar laughed, and John reached over to clap him on the back. Pool balls cracked. The rain came down. The fire clanked and fell into itself. One of the men got up to throw in another log.

As the storm intensified, they got up a pool tournament in the tavern, setting the candles right on the bumpers. People kept coming in. The telephone linesman pulled in, figuring it was safer to hide out in the tavern than to ride a cherry picker in the storm. A woman named Annie drove back to the tavern after a tree fell over her lane. Monica and Mike, John's kids, couldn't get home to Hoquiam, so they spent the night by the woodstove. Wind blew the fire back down the stovepipe sometimes, spraying sparks.

"When people stopped coming in," John said, "we knew the North Fork'd cut us off. We tuned an old battery radio to KUKN Cookin' Country, *Well I'm an eight ball shooting double-fisted drinking son of a gun,* and we're all singing along. People are dancing, gusts are banging at the siding, and that wind is hooting across the chimney like it was a long-neck bottle."

John rested on his elbows, grinning.

Rocks

BENSON, ARIZONA

I don't go into caves. They scare the bejeezus out of me. The earth moves. That is a fact. Openings slide shut. Rocks fall. "You'll have to go some distance to get me into a cave," I tell my daughter. And then she does. She announces that her entire wedding party is going to hike in the cave, and the family will be invited as the guests of her new mother-in-law. This is too cruel.

Understand how nice it is on top of the hill. Under a blue sky, cold and clear, yellow rabbitbrush still glows, even with a brush of snow in its shadow. The barrel cactus are fat and shiny with rain. Cactus wrens are churring. The wind smells of wood smoke and sage. And then, right in the middle of this paradise, there's a thick metal door into the side of the mountain, like the door to a bank vault or the entrance to hell. This is where we go in.

Okay, I say to myself. You are able to go through a door. Tour guides close it behind us, and here is a long concrete-lined passageway with another door at the far end. Okay, you've changed terminals at O'Hare; you can go through an underground tunnel. There's the second door. Okay. You can do it; a door is just a door. They close that one behind me. I wheel around to make sure I know how to open the latch, even in the dark. Okay. But suddenly I can't breathe. The air is too wet. How wet can air be, before you drown in it? I suck in my breath. The lights go off behind us. My daughter holds my hand. Okay. It's okay.

Simultaneously, lights go on in front of us, and we are in a vast high-vaulted cavern made of stone that glistens like sugar. Pillars delicate as soda straws reach to a ceiling that seems to be sliding in sparkling shields down the walls and dripping light from each point and fault. The floor falls away in glowing moon-milk terraces then rises suddenly to a throne studded with stars. A fin of rock glows blue as a glacier.

I had no idea. I had no idea there was an astonishing world inside the scratchy hill. I had imagined the cave was made of dirt, not glass. The others wander on, but I find myself just standing there. I start after them, afraid to be left behind. But then I stop, because maybe all I want is to be alone in this vast, shining silence. I lean on the railing and wait. A drop of water falls into a pool. Tock. Another. Pock. Water rings against rock and echoes through the hall. Water chimes against stone and sings like glass.

I didn't know there was such music in these hills. I didn't know I was crying. So much takes me by surprise.

Hills

The road goes gently up a hill between two rows of white pines. Everything—the road, the hill, the pines—is blanketed in snow. The snow is blue this late at night, except where a flake catches some stray cosmic light and glistens white, and except for our tracks, which are white as well. The sky is black and almost too cold for stars. We have left the pickup at the gate and trudged up here at least a mile, three women who have only just met. We are going out to sing for wolves.

I have howled for wolves before, often standing at the edge of ice in the dark, alternately caterwauling and listening, trying to arouse a territorial response from across the night-bound lake. But this is different. Locals already know that there is a family of wolves denning a few miles up the road. We don't need to find them. Instead, our job is to count the pups. So here we are in our boots and mittens and mufflers, hiking through the dark toward a family of wolves, trying to make no sound at all, but our boots are squeaking like mice on the cold snow. I wouldn't mind squeaking like a lumberjack or a hunter, but our sound is distinctly wee and succulent. If a wolf were to stalk us, we would never see it in the deep wells of darkness under the trees, and we would never hear it over the rhythmic creak of our boots.

"Maybe," I say, "we could hold hands," and so we do, finding some comfort as our moist mittens freeze together.

We tromp along. Under the snow, the hill slopes smoothly away on both sides of the trail. Once we startle an owl from its perch. We stop to watch it sail over its star-shadow. We walk more slowly as we get closer to where Pam thinks the wolves will be, so we don't disturb them. At last, she signals us to stop. We stand quietly until even the memory of the sound of our movement fades away. She mouths one, two, three, to remind us that we are to count small voices. Then Pam begins to sing.

She sings a soft sound, as if a mother were trying to put a baby to sleep. The song wanders up and down a minor scale, a tuneless lullaby. Then right at our feet, high-pitched cries—one, two, but I have no idea how many pups are yipping, and "oh my god, we're too close," and we are stumbling backward down the trail.

We run several hundred yards before Pam stops us, and we stand panting in a night gone still. The voices of the pups have fallen away. The trees open in front of us. The black night domes over our heads. Stars glimmer in the snow. In that deep quiet, I can hear the sounding joy, belling across the snow-bound hills, and I don't know if it's the hills resounding or if it's my own heart that is ringing for joy.

> Is the violin's music in the wind or in the wood? Is the bell song in the dome or the tongue? Is the river's *alegria* in the water or in the stones? Is the wind's song in the aspens or in the human exultation? Is music a wellspring, or is it the drinking of its water? Trick questions, all of them. Music is the unity of wind and wood, the coming together of what had been apart— dome and tongue, water and stones—the reunion of nature's flowing song and the thirsty spirit.

Night wind shakes the stars in the trees, snow sings off the slope of the hill, wolves hum to their pups, and the depth of the universe throbs like a gong. Somewhere in this same night, choirs raise their voices, *Joy to the World,* shivering the candle flames in the great cathedrals, and mothers sing the words softly to their children after they turn off the lights. While fields and floods / rocks, hills, and plains / Repeat the sounding joy.

Repeat the sounding joy. The more hollow a heart, the more resonant it can become. I would make of this body, this life, a sounding board, tuned to that sympathetic vibration, which is sympathy, which is feeling together, which is compassion for all the world.

Plains

Saskatoon, Saskatchewan

The year our daughter was born, we rode the train from Vancouver to Ohio for Christmas. We had a tiny berth, with two bunk beds and a window the length of the room. It was dark when we set out from the city. I remember lying on my side with Erin cupped in the curve of my body. I watched the red and green and yellow lights of the city give way to moonlight on the cliffs of the Fraser River Canyon. All the evergreens were weighted down with snow, and the river, far below us, was a silver thread through white drifts. The whistle of our train's engine sounded in front of us sometimes, sometimes above us, sometimes behind, always far away. We climbed into the Rockies in the early morning, white snow falling heavily, white through the white trunks of the aspens against the white sky. A single cross-country skier, wearing a red sweater, stood at a railroad crossing.

Our baby was crying, pulling at her ears. We knew she was in pain, and I remember how worried we were, so far from home. I bundled her close and tried to nurse her as the train descended onto the plains, and the dark descended, and the snow fell and fell. Then we were moving through the night across endless snow-blanketed plains, dark except for a white tunnel of light from the train's headlamp, visible when the train made a broad curve to the south. Then there was nothing for miles and miles but darkness and a crying child, and the rhythmic rumble of the train. I sang Christmas carols to her, *and heaven and nature sing,* and rocked her in the rhythm of the thump and drop of the wheels. After a long time, she stopped crying and went to sleep.

For hours, I held her close and watched snow blow from the darkness against the window of the train. I must have slept, and when I awoke I could see small globes of yellow light glowing through the snow, lamplight thrown from the windows of farmhouses evenly spaced across the plains, coming together and moving apart as the train approached and passed. At every crossroads, bells rang and the train sang out, and I could imagine that the people in the little houses felt themselves warm and glad to hear the music from the snow-muffled night.

The Possum in the Plum Tree

I have elected to sleep outside my friend's Oregon farmhouse to-night. I'm lying in my sleeping bag in the purple wetness of the meadow, wakeful and restless, listening to the click and chirr of possums in the plum·tree, hoping that the possums, when they walk home, will not walk across my face. A possum's claws are sharp, and who knows where that tail has been.

If you let possums stay in a plum tree all night, they will eat up all the plums. Then they will come down. Those are the facts. We can fancy them up, talk about the way a possum's head is all mouth—like needle-nose pliers, sharp rows of pinpoint teeth—and how a possum turns its head to get a sideways bite. Maybe there is moon-glow on the plums, a purple smudge between the red river-glints of the possum's eyes. That's all you can see of their work, red eyeshine now and then behind the leaves. If there are no cars passing on the road, you can hear them eat, not possum-lip smacking, because possums curl their lips away from the leaking juice, but teeth clicking against pits—an unexpected politesse.

How can this be, the rightful owner of the orchard will ask when she comes with a plastic pail in the morning. Of course, by then the possums will be gone, and there it will be, the fruitless tree with its folded leaves and maybe a few trails heading away through dewy grass. Did the possums take every one? What could they be thinking? Of course, you will answer, possums think in their ways, but they don't know what they're thinking. It's all just hunger and plum musk and the dead weight of that tail, sticking straight out, and maybe the scrabble of naked babies against belly, the sudden tug and suck.

They're like rats, she will say, and you will say: maybe. Because you know who possums are really like, how they think the world is made for them.

For a possum to leave some plums for the wasps, it would have to imagine wasp hunger, the night-blind wandering toward sweetness, the taste of it on wasp feet. But possum awareness is all a possum knows, and why should it think there is any other kind of knowing or any other hunger quite as sharp? For all it knows (and, of course, it understands very little), the smell of plums and the blue glow of objects at night are the only awareness in the world. Granted, it's a puzzle that sometimes a part of the world stands up and shouts and throws stones. But through it all, the lonely spark of possum-knowing, without any imagination whatsoever, dangles from branches that it never doubts were created to match the curl of its tail.

I know what I'm talking about. I once shook a young possum and yelled at it, informing it in no uncertain terms that it should not have bitten my hand. It played possum. If I were that possum, I would have passed out from embarrassment too, to have made such a fundamental mistake. This was the hand that fed it, after all, that made it a shoebox nest on the bottom shelf of the kitchen cupboard and let it hide back there, eating cat food and pooping in rags. An orphan, it grew stronger each day, and each day stupider. A baby possum at least knows how to cuddle, but a grown-up possum does not.

Just beyond the meadow, the hill rises steeply. That's where the man who owns the hillside found two juvenile vultures in a dank cavern below a rock ledge and fallen tree. I could crawl there from here, if I didn't mind scratches, through tunnels that the mountain beavers have cut in blackberry thickets and slash. The man came upon the cave unexpectedly, from the top, when he was scouting the route for a new trail. He knelt down and looked into the ammoniac darkness. The vulture babies lunged at him, hissing and making to vomit, and he tumbled on his back into the blackberry canes.

The vultures will be grown and gone now. There will be meadow voles in the cave instead, tunneling through black soil made by worms from decades of vulture feces and vomitus. The voles will be chewing on leftover bones, their big eyes shining in the dark, their teeth flashing, drawn toward the flaking calcium, wary of the accumulated death, running in circles, the rodent equivalent to internal debate.

When I went to the Internet to find out more about juvenile vultures, I was led straight to www.Jesus-is-lord.com. As well as I can remember, it said approximately this:

> The vulture is a useful animal. It eats dead animals that would otherwise spread disease. Some vultures eat only bones, swallowing bones longer than their necks and then waiting patiently for the stomach acid to eat away the lower end. If two babies are born, the larger will usually kill and eat the other. God gave us the vulture.

Oh for crying out loud, I thought. God is trying to figure out how to get rid of disease and dead animals for us, and he decides to make baby birds that kill each other in their cribs, then stalk around with femurs sticking out of their throats like carrots in a garbage disposal. I could as easily believe that God made us to serve the vultures. Slaughtering sheep and pigs, running over possums on the road, smashing into unimaginative deer, floating the corpses of our loved ones down the river—we do our duties to vultures better than vultures do their duties to us.

I thought about that, but not for long. I assume that the vulture takes all these moldering gifts for granted. A vulture mind seems acid-sour to me, sharply self-absorbed, sluggish with a gizzard full of its sister's bones. But I can only guess.

The night is so wet that the stars are white smudges and the thin crescent of the moon is fuzzy as a slipper. I fold the ground cloth over my sleeping bag to fend off some of the damp. Wetness carries smells and muffles sounds, so I don't know if what I hear is the thrumming of the creek or of a ruffed grouse, but surely what I smell is all creek—algae and that randy smell of willow leaves left out in the rain. I see the silhouette of the hill's slope from the corners of my eyes. It is important that I not move my head. The sopping edge of sleeping bag closest to my face is warm. But if I turn, the fabric slaps me like lettuce.

The rationalist philosopher René Descartes believed that humans are the only conscious beings in the universe. Oh, there are the usual urgings and imperatives and shufflings toward food and female must. There is cringing and striking out, just as there is rolling downhill and striking rock. But humans alone can hear themselves think. This is what he says.

I don't know how to respond. He's got to be partly right. Humans *are* different from the rest of creation. Could a vulture invent football? Could a human disarticulate a cow's bones with his lips? But even given our difference from other animals, surely it's a kind of possum-stupidity, when you know only your own mind, to deny the existence of all other minds.

It doesn't work for me. I'm a pragmatist. If an idea has disastrous consequences in the world, that's pretty good evidence that it isn't true. And the idea that humans can lord it over the Earth because they have conscious minds hasn't worked for, oh, say two thousand years, as humans skimmed the Earth for whatever they want, leaving less and less for the stone-dumb others and finally, now, wondering where they will find sustenance in a world stripped of its fruit.

But Descartes needed to believe that we—we alone—are the only thinking, creative substance in the universe, because if that's true, if we are that special, then it is possible to believe that we are the only beings of true value of the universe and that all the value of the universe derives from us.

But I'd rather listen to my friends Mary Evelyn Tucker, who is a theologian, and Brian Swimme, a cosmologist. Here's what they tell me, making it simple for my sake.

We are not:

The purpose of the universe.

The universe does not:

Exist for our sakes.

I am lying on my back in a meadow in the dark, looking up. Possums are companionably chewing in the tree beside me. Voles are licking their tails up the hill. On this damp night, I could make myself believe that I'm the center of the universe. This is a pretty cozy place. I count maybe two dozen stars in a dome that seems no bigger than necessary to enclose this exact meadow. Plato, a smart but deluded man, believed that the universe was so small that if all the people in the world shouted at the same time, they could hear their voices echo back from the dome of the universe. But I know that if I shouted, the vibration of my voice would sail into the dark night, fading until it ran out of air or by some chance bumped into a cloud and snuffed out.

"Help!" I shout.

Nothing.

See?

Quod erat demonstrandum.

Here's how Mary Evelyn and Brian have helped me think about it. Almost fourteen billion years ago, the infinitely small point that was everything exploded, slinging out dust and light in every direction. Over unimaginable expanses of time, the dust started to accrete. It spun out galaxies, and galaxies spun out stars, and the stars, planets: creation unfurling, the way a peony unfurls, layer after layer of translucent petals. The creative universe is perfect. If dust and light blew out more quickly, they would disperse forever; if more slowly, the matter of the universe would collapse into yet another infinitely dense point of beginning. Instead, the elements of the stars came together to create silver willows, spirochetes, tall fescue, crickets, my febrile mind and all the other minds, vibrating between matter and energy, which we often (in our self-absorbed way) call life and death.

What this means is that I don't have to think of myself as the lonely king of the universe, a young Alexander or aging Napoleon, trusting no one, and for very good reason. Honestly, if that's what I thought—that I and my kind were the only sparks of awareness in the whole dead universe—I would never sleep out under the stars for fear that the alien darkness would float me like cold water, and I would flail frantically like a single spark from a fire and wink out in the fog. No. I doze on wet grass and imagine myself part of the mysterious unfolding of the universe, imagine that inflorescence. I fit in here. Literally.

I am one unfolding among other interfoldings and enfoldings, the wrinkled lap and pucker of life in Earth, the vulture and the possum and the dew on the plums.

For how smart we think we are, how facile with words, we don't have a word for this feeling, the feeling of being blessed by belonging. If the universe is an unfolding bud, then I am a part of its creative surge, along with the flowing of water and the growing of pines. I can find a kind of camaraderie in this universe, once I recover from the astonishment of it. Or maybe not camaraderie exactly. What is the opposite of loneliness?

The Time for the Singing of Birds

*For lo, the winter is past. The rain is over and gone. The
flowers appear on the earth. The time for the singing of
birds has come.*
— Song of Solomon

This is a story a friend gave to me. I am giving it to you.

There was a man who searched and searched for the sacred in
nature—in the forest, at the beach—and sure enough: one day as
he was walking along the coast, he heard a voice, loud and clear.

"Stand here," it said, "and God will speak to you."

The man stood. What else could he do? What would you have
done? He stood for a very long time, shifting his weight from one leg
to the other. His back stiffened up. A flock of brants flew down the
trough between the breakers. The wind came up and died back. The
tide flowed in. He zipped his jacket and unzipped it, zipped it again,
as the sun went down and gulls cried out and flew to their roosts. He
shivered in fog that came with night, and finally he went home.

· I'm not sure what he hoped to hear. The sound of wind bringing rain, the rattle of surf-driven stones—didn't these tell him what he needed to know? That he is alive in this place, at this time, alive in the midst of all this life. That he is aware in the midst of all that is mysterious, every fact that might not have been and yet is. Stinging sand, the storm-driven waves, the swirling gulls—they are all cause for surprise and celebration.

Instead of standing still and waiting for instructions, what if he had laid on his back in the midst of the mussels, laid there with barnacles poking his scalp, felt—in the hollow echo chamber of his ribs—the breakers pound against rock, listened to the shouts of faraway children and the pop of sand fleas next to his ear, as all the while tide crept in around him and surf exploded closer and closer to his brain?

Then what would he have heard?

I don't want to say he would have heard the voice of God.

I want to say he would have heard—really heard, maybe for the first time—the squeak of mussels, the smash of surf, the peeping of sandpipers. Maybe a fish crow cawing or a chainsaw cutting cedar drifted in on storms. ·

And I want to say that this is enough. I want to say that this is astonishing enough—the actual Earth, the extraordinary fact of the ticking, smashing, singing, whistling, peeping Earth—to make me feel that I live in a sacred place and time.

I want to say that there is a secular sacred, that this phrase, paradoxical as it seems, makes good and profoundly important sense.

Here is what I believe: that the natural world—the stuff of our lives, the world we plod through, hardly hearing, the world we burn and poke and stuff and conquer and irradiate—that THIS WORLD (not another world on another plane) is irreplaceable, astonishing, contingent, eternal and changing, beautiful and fearsome, beyond human understanding, worthy of reverence and awe, worthy of celebration and protection.

If the good English word for this combination of qualities is "sacred," then so be it. Even if we don't believe in God, we walk out the door on a sacred morning and lift our eyes to the sacred rain and are called to remember our sacred obligations of care and celebration.

And what's more, if the natural world is sacred, and "sacred" describes the natural world; if there are not two worlds but one, and it is magnificent and mysterious enough to shake us to the core; if this is so, then we—you and I and the man on the beach—are called to live our lives gladly. We are called to live lives of gratitude, joy, and caring, profoundly moved by the bare fact that we live in the time of the singing of birds.

Gladness lifts the natural world out of the merely mundane and makes it wonderful, and reminds us that when we use the sacred stuff of our lives for human purposes, we must do so gratefully and responsibly, with full and caring hearts. That's what I want to say.

My mother and father were biologists. When I was growing up, there were sprouting beans tied to the hands of the clock, growing in circles as time revolved. Fairy shrimp flutter-kicked through jars of pond water on the sunlit window sills, butterfly eggs hatched in the living room, little mirrors angled over bird nests so we could see the babies without disturbing the nest, a frozen woodpecker rested in the freezer for reasons that escape me now, purple eggplants were grafted with white polka dots.

Everything in the house gloried in the moment, the fact of things. Everything focused on how things are, and why, and how wonderful. All the joy-filled facts. All the astonishing connections.

All the irresistible questions. We went to church on Sunday mornings, but in the afternoons, we traipsed through bogs and creeks and buzzing meadows, tapping stones against dead trees to call in downy woodpeckers.

And now I'm married to a biologist. You should see us in a canoe in the dark—philosopher in the bow, biologist in the stern. I'm rejoicing in the sounds of the night, awash in metaphors, and Frank is explaining the biomechanics of frog song.

"Imagine blowing up a balloon," he says.

"Now imagine blowing up a balloon made of your neck skin.

"Now imagine blowing it up twice your size.

"Now hold that and tremble all night.

"The energetics of this music are so tough, so much energy expended, that it could kill a frog. Some tree frogs have only enough energy to sing for three nights. Three trembling nights. Imagine that.

"Imagine the silence of the frogs on day four."

I sit quietly, imagining. What else can I do?

Then Frank says, "Now imagine swallowing a moth so big that you have to push it down your throat with your eyeballs."

And then we look across the lake, where the path of the moon glitters on the discarded wings of a trillion flying ants. We look at the moon itself, bulging out between black mountains. And we note in passing that we ourselves are sailing at however many zillion miles per hour through the darkness, spinning in a spiral galaxy slung across space, slung out with all the singing frogs and the quiet ones, all of us up to our eyeballs in swamp.

And if we even think about our own sparking minds on that sparkling lake, the molecular structure of awareness, the biochemistry of celebration, the universe singing its own praises in the languages of philosophy and science, then we have to hold on to keep from falling out of the canoe. Astonished, yes. And shaken.

The secular sacred. Secular: living in the world. Sacred: worthy of reverence and awe. Reverence: profound respect mixed with love and awe. Awe: fear and admiration.

Some people suggest that science is the enemy of the sacred. This puzzles me. I suppose the argument is that the more we understand or think we understand, the smaller the realm of mystery becomes; under the hot lights of scientific knowledge, the sacred warps and shrinks, like Styrofoam in flames. But this argument won't work because mystery is infinite, the only natural resource that humans can't exhaust in this giant fire sale we call an economy.

The physicist Chet Raymo thinks of scientific understanding as an island in a sea of mystery. The larger the island, the longer its coastline—that area where the deep sea of what we don't understand slaps and smacks at the edge of what we think we know, a rich place of bright water and dark, fecund smell.

If so, then this is our work in the world: to pull on rubber boots and stand in this lively, dangerous water, bracing against the slapping waves, one foot on stone, another on sand. When one foot slips and the other sinks, to hop awkwardly to keep from filling our boots. To laugh, to point, and sometimes to let this surging, light-flecked mystery wash into us and knock us to our knees, while we sing songs of celebration through our own three short nights, our voices thin in the darkness.

If I Hadn't Stopped to Watch the River

It's not as warm as I had hoped, here on the east side of the Cascades. High clouds over the mountains have kept the morning sun from hitting the ponderosas. With snow only just gone, dirt crumbles in lumpy, frost-built castles. Pine needles crosshatch the trail, gray under amber. All the same, green moss grows where springs flow into the river, and chartreuse lichens blown off the trees by winter storms litter the trail. Walking along the river, I hear fly fishers' lines zing, and robins at every turn sing their chirruping morning songs. I should be happy, but I find myself hurrying down the trail. Already, just a few hours into the weekend, time feels short. I hurry to relax before I have to go back to my complicated life.

My complicated life, or maybe I should say, my impossible life. I think what I do is right, and maybe even important sometimes, or maybe not. But the point is, there's too much of it—too much and a sense of never having a chance to lift my eyes to the horizon. In fact, there is no horizon visible from our house; it's all shelter and no prospect, with telephone lines and neighbors' roofs crowding out the sky. There's no horizon visible from my life either. All the projects crowd around, so close I can't see past them and the damnable computer screen. I can't imagine the future. It's hard enough getting through the day.

Under a dead old ponderosa, I sit on ground scaled with jigsaw flakes of bark, pull out a pencil, and open my journal. What a relief to get away from town. What a relief finally to have time to write a to-do list. "To do," I write, and add a colon: Syllabus. Note to Jan. Report to Courtney. Regrets to Tim. Proposal for turtle book. Fat ants. Pine log weathered into gray cubes. Cedar fronds tipped with pollen. Green grass emerging from last year's towhead tufts, all cowlicks and warm sun. Cold wind. Slick river. Pond weeds marking the current. Two river otters.

I put down my pencil and watch the otters feed in fast water near the far bank. They are small ones, maybe young ones, lifting in smooth curves over the riffles, porpoising in perfect synchrony. That's odd: otters *porpoise*. An animal can become a verb to describe a different animal's action. This could be fun. I lift my pencil again, thinking of other animal names we use for verbs, and I come up with a list of verbs longer than I expected. Weasel. Bull. Buffalo and cow. Goose and duck. "She goosed him, then ducked." Horse around and pig out and cat around. Skunk. Snake. Dog. Pony up, rat on, ferret out, and wolf down. Lots of animals are ways to be. So how would I describe my life? *Squid*: "Finishing her lecture and closing her notebook, she squidded out of the classroom." Or *octopus*: "She sits in her office, phone and appointment book close at hand, and octopies her life away." What would it be simply to *human*? "She vowed that the next morning, she would make time to human."

It feels good just to sit and watch the river. I will my mind to be still, but that's sort of a joke. *Still* is not something I'm good at, and the fact disturbs me a great deal. "The moments when the mind is absorbed by beauty are the only hours when we really live. All else is illusion or mere endurance." This is the British naturalist Richard Jeffries, and what if he's right? One thing follows for sure: if I'm obsessing about the meaning of Richard Jeffries, then by his standards I'm not alive. And this blue river, rushing by bare soil and yellow grass just exposed by spring: isn't it telling me the same thing? Every time the river rubs around a rock, picking up speed and scattering, it loses all color. Water turns pale in the fast places, the way the rainbow of a trout fades when it dies. Only in the deepest pools and quietest water does the river saturate with blue.

A flock of butterflies wings in to drink from a patch of mud so close to me that I have to stand up and walk a few steps back to bring binoculars into focus. California tortoiseshells, I think. This is an unusual sighting. Tortoiseshells appear only one in three or five years, and no one knows much about them— whether they go somewhere else in the interval or whether they need three years for the next generation to hatch. At any rate, this turns out to be the right place and the right year, and I feel lucky to be with butterflies on this steep slope down to the river, under ponderosa pines in this rare sun.

And then the really lucky thing: a tortoiseshell floats close to me, tilts around my face as if it were trying to read my mind, and then lands on my arm. I can see its shiny dot eyes and curled antennae. The hairs on its back flow under the wind. I fight the urge to stroke its back like a dog's. The butterfly walks up my arm, almost to my elbow, and unrolls its tongue, a fine black thread as long as its bandy legs. It touches its tongue to my arm. A butterfly is tasting me. Is it the salt on my skin? This is a good day.

I stand without moving for a very long time, and still the butterfly touches me with its tongue. So much time goes by that my feet start to burn in their boots. I sit down very, very slowly, holding my arm at precisely the right angle. The butterfly keeps tonguing as I sit cross-legged on the trail.

Here's a possible meaning for the verb "to human": to provide salt for the California tortoiseshell butterfly. Maybe all the other things I might have accomplished or thought I ought to do, maybe they are the illusions, the flutter-stuff, the lead-up to the main show—which is to sit still and watch an insect lick my arm on a day barely past winter.

Now the tortoiseshell climbs higher up my arm until it's almost to my shoulder, so close to my eyes that I can't focus on it. Even so, I sit without moving: if this is my leading role in life, I don't want to flub it. Then I very, very slowly fish for my glasses in the pocket of the jacket tied around my waist. I worm them out, inch by inch—hard to do, since I am sitting on them. Now I can see the tortoiseshell perfectly, a foot from my eyes. It's dark orange like old peels, with a fringed black border and soft brown spots. It holds its wings down, barely touching my arm, to keep the wind from blowing it away.

Lucky. If I hadn't stopped to watch the river, if I hadn't worked up a sweat in this unlikely sun, if I hadn't pushed my sleeves up past my elbows, I might never have discovered how to drink in the peace of this time and place, every warm drop.

In an ancient forest not far from this one, I met a man who was writing a book about the end of humankind. He didn't know how human beings would disappear. Whether we would all perish in a plague, or blow ourselves up with nuclear weapons, or die from the poisons we spread, or rise on angel's wings flapping in the blasts of trumpets—he didn't know or much care. His book is about what the Earth does next, how the forest grows when no one cuts it, exactly how a building falls apart and a dam erodes, what trace of us will be left a hundred years after we are all gone, a thousand.

"Well," I tossed out. "There will be a few good months for the condors." But then the vision of shadows cast by condors over the bloated forms sobered me. "You are writing a sad book," I said, but he didn't think so.

"What will Earth lose, when it loses human beings?" he challenged me. The question was genuine, and I took it seriously. I thought of joy first, but he wouldn't give me that, arguing that animals feel joy, and I think that's right, as anyone would who has watched young crows play in updrafts. Then I thought of music. But Earth is full of music, he said; and if I'm thinking of Bach, which I was, then the fugues are still there in vibrations sailing away from Earth, as they will sail forever, along with everything the Beatles sang and every baseball game.

It's the awareness of these, I thought then. Not just joy, but the awareness of joy. Not just music, but that swelling response to music, the way it opens the heart. Humans are Earth's way of knowing itself. With the tongue of a human being, Earth tastes itself. In a human's search for meaning, it comes to know its own mysteries. In a human's loving attention, Earth rejoices in its own beauty. It's one thing to be. It's quite another to know that and to pronounce it good. This is what a human brings to the world—the ability to take notice, to be grateful and glad, glad for the river swinging by, for the sun warming my shoulders, for the breeze lifting the hairs on a butterfly's back.

Courage

Look, the Rain Has Stopped

There is no mercy in this rain. It falls hard on my college town, it falls loud, it falls for three days and nights unceasing. Low, dusky clouds weigh on my students' shoulders and rest heavily on their spirits. Classroom windows steam up, increasing the gloom. Rainwater drains across the classroom floor, fed by streams flowing steadily from black and orange umbrellas. The room smells of wet plaster and damp wool.

Sidewalks flood, forcing students to high-step through lawns already so sodden that each footprint fills with water. Soccer fields flood. Parking lots flood. Storm drains flood. Oak Creek runs high and muddy. I walk to school in the dark, walk home in the dark, and teach with wet feet, raising my voice over the din. I lecture about the British philosopher Thomas Hobbes, who pronounced the lives of men "solitary, poor, nasty, brutish, and short." The human condition is like bad weather, he wrote, hammered not so much by rain and storm as by the fear of them.

The weather man calls this storm a Pineapple Express because it rolls into campus from the South Pacific, loaded with water—a black freight train rumbling past the humanities building with sullen disregard, day after day after day.

In the second week of the term, the town wakes up to a silver thaw. All through the day, oak limbs crack and thunder to earth in a flurry of ice and robins. Ice coats every laurel leaf, every branch of every oak and bundle of mistletoe, every stop sign and sidewalk. The whole world shines. "Warm rain is falling through cold air," says the radio announcer, and the university closes to protect the students. It is too dangerous to drive, even if people *could* open their car doors through a half inch of ice. I cancel my lecture on the Enlightenment idea of continuous progress. Then, pulling on a parka, I skid out to see.

Rain continues to fall, building ice-knobs on the buds of dogwood trees, outlining azaleas with light, transforming rose thorns into glass swords. Even as I watch, the weight of the ice becomes too much for an old Douglas-fir in the next block. With a great crackling, a limb falls through the lower branches and smashes into the street, taking down an electric wire through a cloud of sparks and smoke. Still the rain falls. By the time this silver thaw is over, campus is a tangle of split limbs and littered branches.

Soon after, a squall blows into campus from the coast range, a short-lived commotion of wind-driven rain. This kind of rain moves in fast and hits hard, almost always during the time between classes. I am preparing a lecture on *The Stranger*. "Look," Mersault says, "The rain has stopped," and he walks home, telling no one of a particular splash he has heard at the Pont Neuf, which may or may not have been a woman leaping into the Seine.

From my second-story office window, I watch one student running awkwardly through sheeting rain. Dressed in a T-shirt and jeans, he gallops with his head down, his notebook clasped to his chest. Another student strolls along the brick walk, completely oblivious to the rain. Two women cut the difference, hurrying across the space between buildings, their backpacks bouncing, their arms crossed, annoyance in their stride.

When you're caught in a squall without a parka, it's hard to know if you should walk or run. If you walk between buildings, the rain has a longer chance to soak you, flattening your hair and running in rivulets down your forehead. If you run, you shorten the time you're exposed to the rain, but you collide with the raindrops full force, driving them down your neck and wetting your pant legs, and this is especially miserable—jeans sticking to your knees, cold and clammy all through class.

In other college towns, the soft rain falling now might be called drizzle, but that doesn't credit the kindness of this rain. Soft rain falls at exactly the rate that can be absorbed by green mats of moss and sweet layers of pine duff, exactly the rate that Douglas-firs and Sitka spruce can pull it into their shining needles, exactly the rate that water evaporates from a person's hair. Students stand in soft rain and never get wet. Meanwhile, all around them, grass fields grow green, trees lengthen and put on girth, frogs sing as if their hearts would burst, and along the roads, Scotch broom blooms over yellow hills.

Soft rain smells like apples. It tastes like pine trees. In class, against the windows, it sounds like somebody shushing a child. The subject today is existentialism. Existence is not a necessity, Sartre wrote. What is, might not have been. Your life, all lives, are facts without explanation. "When you realize that, it turns your heart upside down and everything begins to float."

In the quad, a student lies on her back in soft rain, licking moisture off her face. When she stands up, there is an outline of her body, light against dark pavement—a rain angel.

Finally, in the fifth week, here is the rain that falls like light through trees just beginning to green. On a rare day of sunlit sky, white clouds ramble eastward, trailing showers. These are the days of rainbows, double rainbows, triple rainbows, arching over the entire campus from the grass fields in the south to the fir-clothed hills to the north. Sidewalks steam. The cupola of the music building glows in storm light, and every fleck of rain shines like glitter, floating. I can hear a trumpet climbing the musical scales, up and up, and when a car drives by, the music is the Beach Boys. Not all my students show up in class today to hear my lecture about Descartes, who could imagine his head was a cabbage but could not imagine he didn't exist.

The Weather Beaver, the little icon that forecasts weather in our local paper, calls this "broken sun." I don't know why. It might mean that the sunny expanse of the day may be broken by showers, but these showers do no damage to the sun. I like to think it means that on a day like this, the sun, expanding, flies apart into a million flecks of light that drift onto the sports fields, the fir trees, the uplifted faces of the students.

In the sixth week, I walk home late, having finished my evening class on Spinoza. "Things could have been produced by God in no other way, and in no other order than they have been produced." With my hood up against the rain, I step carefully through deep puddles, leaves slippery on the sidewalk. Rain hits hard, dashing on the pavement, sheeting up from passing cars, each car a sweep of light through the rain, then deeper dark. Someone on my neighbor's patio is kneeling down and pumping, as all the neighbors are pumping something in these torrential rains, trying to clear water from a gutter or a low place in the garden.

But this is my neighbor's son kneeling stiff-armed over his father, pressing against the old man's chest, then forcing air through the grimace of his mouth, pressing all his weight against his father's heart and leaning back to let his heart suck open again. I hear sirens, too far away and not coming fast enough. I put my arm around the shoulders of my neighbor's wife and grip her hard as she prays.

What I will always remember is how rain falls from black sky through the streetlight onto my neighbor splayed out on concrete. His shirt is torn open, and his bare chest is shiny with rain. The red lights of the ambulance flash in the water on his chest, which isn't rising and falling but lying slick and solid, luminous with rain, casting a hard black shadow on the ground.

Up in the mountains for a field course, I wake to the splatter of rain on my tent. I know that my Philosophy of Nature students are lying in their own tents in various degrees of wakefulness, girding themselves against yet another day of rain. They will pull on parkas still damp from the day before and gather under the tarp that covers the fire pit and a ring of camp chairs. They will stand there talking and laughing quietly, each one hunched over a small cloud of steam from a cup of coffee. Wood smoke will river around their feet, and the flames will warm their backs and dry their coats. They will be glad to be together.

I will gather my books and a cup of tea, and I will join the students under the tarp. I think I will teach about mystery today, this bright ocean that surrounds the small island of our understanding, the rain that rises from that sea.

I don't know why we live or die, whether that's necessary or contingent. But I will tell my students this: life and death are all or nothing. When you die, it's done, the chance is gone. So when you live? When you live, make it all. Don't wait for the rain to stop. Climb out of your tent with your mind engaged and your senses ablaze and let rain pour into you. Remember: you are not who you think you are. You are what you do. Be the kindness of soft rain. Be the beauty of light behind a tall fir. Be gratitude. Be gladness.

After a time, I hear the creak of the pump handle, the thump of the outhouse door. A slosh as someone launches a canoe. Wood snapping, sticks breaking, and then the smell of wood smoke on damp wind. Two students talk quietly by the fire. I think I smell coffee, but it may be the damp earth.

Twenty Things Morning Reveals

1. That a hard freeze fell over the sand dunes at the Oregon coast last night. In morning light, our tent shines under the skim of ice, and the teapot clangs like a cow bell when I shake it. Frost has brightened the surface of the dunes, so tracks are written boldly on the sand and signs on the slopes around camp are easy to read.

2. That a frog hopped past before dawn, leaving its marks on the frozen sand. If I kneel, I can see the flapping hind feet and the stars of its open hands. When we heard frogs singing under the sharp stars last night, even as we shivered beside the campfire, we wondered how they could live under a skim of ice. But at least one frog has lived through the night. In the morning light, this is revealed.

3. That if I were to follow the tracks of the possum that passed by last night, I would wander dazed, as if I had been clubbed.

But when I follow the tracks of the little spotted skunk, I walk directly across the sand to the nearest stump, dig under it briefly, then set off straight to the horizon.

4. That my husband was excited, hiking out before dawn to cast a spinner to steelhead. Here are his waffle tracks, the mound of sand pushed behind each footstep. The spring tide will have brought a new flush of fish upriver from the ocean, silver and hard-muscled and eager with eggs. When I cross his tracks, I can read energy in the length of his stride.

5. That deer gathered in the hollow behind the tree island last night. Adults, yearlings, and maybe a deer with a tender foot drove the sharp edges of their hooves deep in the sand as they trotted under the river of stars pouring into the sea.

6. That two coyotes, traveling together toward the river, avoided our camp in the night, one passing to the east, one to the west, like skis around a stump, and joined up again about a hundred feet beyond the tent. Comrades.

7. That porcupines are pigeon-toed, and their belly spines drag.

8. That blowing leaves and sticks create mysterious tracks. I thought, just for a minute: Was this a tarantula with a sprained ankle? Or a magical crow wearing bedroom slippers? I followed the tracks and found a pussy willow twig and a dried alder leaf, its back arched.

9. That beetles plodded along here, even under the coyote's belly. Miniscule eskers wind over the sand, mounds beetles make as they pushed through new tunnels. Where they popped

out into starlight, the mounds became runnels, like tiny river courses.

10. That a bear passed this way some days ago. Here is an old bear track, where its weight compressed the sand into a saucer with fat toes. Then wind must have blown away the surrounding sand, so the track emerged like a mesa in the desert.

11. That anything with weight can make a mountain—here a flake of charcoal, there a hemlock cone, even the wing cover of a beetle. On the ridge above camp, each object stands on a narrow pedestal of sand that the wind did not have the strength to blow away.

12. That the night was cold. Here, under a beach pea, lies the body of a ruby-crowned kinglet so slight I can barely feel his weight in my hand. His tiny bill is open, as if he froze crying out, his threadlike claws clenched, one wing frozen into the feathers on his flank.

13. That the night was clear. This close to the ocean, only a clear night is cold enough to freeze this pattern into the skin of ice on the sand-sink pond, ice crystals creeping from the near bank to the farther shore across shards of black sky and starlight.

14. That the sun has finally cleared the hills. Every tree fills with birdsong the very moment it fills with light.

15. That west is over my right shoulder, past the willows in the deflation plain. Every hillock, every beach grass thicket, every mount of sand points a silvery finger to the west as the early sun melts the frost in all the places but the shadows.

16. That the teakettle is boiling. Even from this sand ridge, I can see the shadow of the steam, wavering on the sand. This morning's tea will be made of frog pond water, and it will taste of life.

17. That there is fire even in the gray-green lichen, the hair grown wild on dead pine limbs. White, light-filled smoke spirals over the campfire.

18. That the tide is going out. Last night, the surf thudded and roared, although we are half a mile from the beach and separated from the waves by a shore pine thicket and a willow swamp. Now, in bright light, the sound is farther away and somehow calmer.

19. That we have lived through the night. While I was dreaming, a huge wave thudded on the beach, so heavy the sand shook even so far inland. I woke up and thought, this is a tsunami. This is the leading edge of a wave raised by a deep-sea earthquake a hundred miles away, and water will surge in after it and snake its way quickly through the low places, and it will rise up and loosen our tent stakes and for a few wild minutes it will float our tent. Then the water will find its way inside and tumble us like a load of laundry, and we will scream and drown. But we didn't. We didn't drown. In the morning light, this is revealed.

20. That my jeans will soon be dry. Frost soaked them when I walked through beach grass before dawn, but steam rises from them now in the warmth of sunlight, as if my legs were smoldering and might any moment burst into flame. I have heard of this, that there are people so filled with surprise and gratitude that they spontaneously ignite and nothing is left of them but ash in a pair of boots.

How Can I Keep from Singing?

Mount St. Helens

Ghost Lake

Ghost Lake Trail forges through the blast zone where the forest took the full force of the Mount St. Helens eruption. Spruce and fir lie where they fell, as if an army of trees, fleeing, had pitched on their faces in the direction of their flight. The blast rolled over them, scorched their limbs, crackled their skin, pressed them into the ash. Rank on rank of shattered tree trunks, half-buried in stones, reach out with broken limbs. The blast must have flanked the mountain and charged down the hillside, burning the slope to stones. Then the hill slid out from under the trees, dropping them in a slag heap of pumice and slash. This is where we're hiking, my friends and I, across this gray and ruined land toward a pond pierced by snags.

My friends are singing. They surprise me. They laugh as

they sing, dredging their memories for the words to an old hymn.

> Through all the tumult and the strife
> I hear the music ringing.

When I stop to listen, I am surprised to hear music too, the thin green pulse of frog song and a winter wren chattering in a huckleberry thicket. I can't see the wren for all the new growth of alder saplings and young firs, poking up from the blanket of blueberry shrubs. An entire forest is rising from the ashes. Chickadees sing from the spiraling branches of silver firs. Between fallen trunks, fireweed and lupine grow lavishly purple and pink, blowsy with seeds. A goldeneye duck stands on one leg at the edge of the pond. And between the drowned snags, my friend wades barefoot, waving her hand in time with the song.

> It finds an echo in my soul—
> How can I keep from singing?

What is this mountain, where hope rides the back of horror, the two of them galloping in such perfect synchrony that they might be one thing? The sorrow or the birdsong: which is the meaning of the mountain? I'm sure that in one second, only that, the blast seared the eyes of a robin that looked over her shoulder in sudden alarm. In the next second, everything was gone but her bones and the silence after the scream. Every bird killed. Every large mammal. Fifty-seven human beings. These are the facts. And not just these, but what they signify: that someday everything I love will be folded back into the earth—that's how Scott Russell Sanders said it. Every person I love, every song I sing, every beloved child, every poem will fold back into the roar of the Earth's fire and disappear forever.

At the same time, in the same place, there is the fact of fireweed. There is the fact of frogs returned, who knows how. Maybe they hopped through the ashes or emerged, blinking, from mud under a snowbank behind a hill. There is the wandering coyote, kicking up dust as it licks for ants and defecates a twist of ash. There are the facts of spider silk tangling in green moss, and blanketing lichen, and beavers trooping down new river courses to chew willows nourished by ash and dust. There must be a lesson here too, maybe exactly this—that no matter how fragile and finite small lives may be, no matter how we grieve our own anticipated deaths, life itself is a powerful force that will not be turned away. But how can we take comfort in that, we mortals who cling to the significance of small lives?

Horse Ridge

We've pitched our tents in pumice on a north-south spine of Mount St. Helens. Snow-crowned Mount Adams floats on forests to the east; to the west, the caldera stands raw and gray. As daylight drains from our camp, pink light collects in the cracked bowl of the volcano. One after another, we set down our coffee cups and gather on the ridge to watch. A pink cloud glows above lavender cliffs and dims the rosy distance. At a sudden rumble of rock, we shout and scramble for binoculars to watch rubble roll down the caldera's flank. A dust plume boils over the rim as the last of the light shafts through broken rock, flickering in red smoke.

I've seen paintings of creation that look like this—a red gleam spreading across smoking stone. And I've seen imaginings of the end of time that look just the same—gray rock seamed with fire, rising smoke, falling darkness, nothing left of life except a handful of human beings lined up at the edge of Destruction, unable to speak.

The smoke stays with me in my dreams—lava boiling down canyons, trapping me on a ridge. In the dark before morning, low rumbling shakes me awake. Light strobes the side of the tent. An eruption? I'm on my knees at the door. But it's lightning that crashes between the mountains. Thunder rolls again, and I unzip the tent. The broken side of the mountain fills the doorway. A bolt of lightning shoots from the crater almost to the moon, half hidden behind storm clouds. Light floods the tent. Thunder shakes the ground under my knees. Should I run down the road to the landing and bring up a van to protect us, all my friends who chose their tent sites for the view? Making camp on the highest ridge for miles around had seemed like such a good idea. I count off seconds to gauge the distance of the storm and turn my head to judge its direction. The lightning might pass to the north. It might not.

In the morning, I pull on a rain slicker and climb out into a cold, wet day. Dawn floods under purple clouds that dash lightning onto the mountains to the north. Wind-driven rain rivers down the road. But sunshine pours over clouds on Mount Adams, and when we gather for breakfast, a meadowlark sings.

Under the flapping tarp that shelters the picnic tables, a geologist hangs on to the tent poles to keep the whole structure from winging across the valley. With his free hand, he gestures wildly toward the crater.

"The gas cloud over the 1980 eruption was full of lightning—zapping up, down, every which way. It charged the nitrogen in the ammonia and ozone. So the ash that fell from the cloud was full of nitrogen that fertilized new plants."

He can hardly contain his excitement at the ecological possibilities of the eruption. And in fact, all the scientists here are

jazzed by what they call this great "biomass disturbance event."
Disturbance kicks the world into motion. What had been stag-
nant is booted into new life. Mature stands of fir and pine are
replaced by meadows and thickets and creek bottoms. What
had been simple is now complex. What had been monochrome
forest is now a hillside of purple lupine and orange butterflies.
What had been silent is noisy with chatter and song.

Destruction, creation, catastrophe, renewal, sorrow, and joy
are merely human ways of seeing, human projections onto the
landscape, the ecologists say. What is real, they say, is change.
What is necessary, they say, is change. Suddenly, there are new
niches, new places to grow and flourish—ponds, landslides,
rocky hillsides, a great profusion of edges where beetles troop
over stumps, huckleberries emerge from snow banks, astonished
pocket gophers dig into the sun. Between the forest patches,
meadows fill with the creatures of wet prairies and oak savan-
nahs.

"Meadowlarks!" an ecologist exults, sweeping his arm toward
the expanse of lupines and corn lilies under the storm. "Where
else can you find meadowlarks on a mountaintop?"

This biomass disturbance has made a new place for birdsong.
I understand that. But at what terrible cost to nestlings burned
in their nests, the sudden silence where there had been hungry
peeping? Lord knows, I'd like to see the world the way ecologists do. If all of us thought of death as change rather than catastrophe, we could blunt the edge of sorrow. And isn't this a source
of hope, that the forces of nature turn death into life again and
again, unceasing?

> Above Earth's lamentation,
> I hear the sweet though far-off hymn
> That hails a new creation.

That's how the song goes. But sometimes I can't hear the hymn for the crying of small birds in the back of my mind.

The Trail from Donnybrook

Climbing through shredded clouds on the trail from Donny-brook, I take small steps across the volcano's landscape of falling. It scares me to walk this trail, one jogging shoe on a rock that must only yesterday have fallen from the mountain, the other on a slope of pumice that trickles down the hill. If I slip, there is nothing that will hold me. The little flower called "'pearly everlasting'" clings to the rubble by what roots? By what hope against reason? And how can it deserve this name—everlasting—with one root in dribbling rubble, the other under a new-fallen stone?

Putting one foot in front of the other across this scratch in the cliff, I lift my hand to block the view of the distance below me to Spirit Lake and the mountains crowding in behind. The lake lies as still as the silence after a car wreck—that still, except for floating tree trunks, bare and gray. They rotate slowly below the wind-driven clouds that curl around the cliff. How do we walk these skidding paths across the edge of an Earth that is tumbling around us? I can hear it go—the clink of cobbles down the face of rough stone. Every step spills sand and stone and bends fireweed to the ground.

I thought I would learn peace from the mountain. Acceptance. I thought I would find comfort in the tenacity of life precariously rooted in constant change. I would learn grace, which I thought was only this: balance as the world slides away under my feet. Instead, I learned how different I am from a mountain, which is not afraid to fall.

Tumbling rocks shake me, body and soul. Falling off rimrock, filling the valleys, the stream of pebbles shakes the belief that human lives are the measure of time. They undercut the conceit that humans are the center of creation, our hopes and sorrows a special concern of Earth's. And what do they say about human pride, the confidence that global events are under human control, that we might understand the Earth and triumph over death? *Ha.* The mountain laughs. *Ha*, a great explosion of ash and steam, jolted by lightning.

But then there is this: Would we fear loss so desperately if we didn't have such a love for the Earth and its life, for our own lives in the midst of indifferent laughter? Would we be afraid of the silence of a robin if a robin's song didn't mean so much to us? Would we be so afraid of our own deaths if we didn't love life so urgently? If there were no love, there would be no loss. I am quite sure about this. But I wonder if it has to work the other way too. If we did not fear or suffer loss, could we claim to feel love? Maybe grace is a kind of balance after all—love and loss creating each other, sorrow defining gladness, gladness giving shape to sorrow, the way the fog that lifts from the valleys between mountains outlines each ridgeline, each silhouette of reaching firs and silvery pumice plains.

How should a person live in a world that erupts catastrophically, sliding down and down? Here's what I will try to do. Especially when I'm grieving, to listen for wrens. When I listen to wrens, to accept that death has shaped their song. To know both the inevitability of change and the urgency of continued life, the power of the Earth that flows out from its center and gathers all life back into its fold. And especially when I'm caught in my human-scaled sense of time and significance, to know that my life is part of the endless flow of fiery rock.

My life flows on in endless song. How can I keep from singing?

Let It All Go (Seven Feathers)

I.

People say the loons leave the Boundary Waters in Minnesota around the middle of September. I'm not looking forward to the morning when I wake up and they're gone. What is a lake without a loon?—lichens and pine trees scrabbling over poor soil, an expanse of blue, a scatter of red maple among white birch suddenly silent and stiff. I listen carefully from my sleeping bag, and when I hear the call of a loon, I am happy in a way that is hard to explain, relieved that the inevitable has been postponed another day, a day all the warmer, because it may be the last warm day.

This morning, the sun filters through the rocky island, spiking rays of light among the pines. Mist rises around the edges of the marsh, and tendrils of fog float above the taut and golden skin of the lake. Three loons rest in their reflections, preening and whistling in whispers. One loon stands on the water, stretches its wings to their full, magnificent length, and trembles through the length of its body, shaking off droplets of water. Curled feathers float on the lake, barely denting the surface.

I launch the canoe and paddle out to gather loon feathers. But I move too quickly, and the feathers swirl in the whirlpools of my paddle and slide out of reach. The loon calls, a single dark tone rising then falling away. When I finally learn to let the canoe drift, the feathers glide toward me, and I can lean over the gunwale to lift a feather from the water. It's black, with two white dots and a slash of white along one edge.

This is the feather of summer—the feather of competition and lust and the howling beauty of loons in full mating plumage. But now, as the birds preen, the bold feathers fall to the water, giving way to the softer colors of winter when the loons will drift on a salt ocean far away, their plumage as gray as the day, barely distinguishable from the turn of a wave or the wake of a seiner with a load of silver fish.

II.

The portage trail is rough—too rough to risk falling with fifty pounds of boat on our shoulders—so we keep our eyes on the path. We slog through a boggy track of purple-slicked water then climb over a slab of granite, down the other side, and across black peat where birch leaves have fallen like gold coins. In a pine swale, orange needles carpet the path, slippery and soft. We carry the canoe across roots that boots have polished to amber and onto soft soil where bracken ferns fall across the way. Pressed into the earth by heavy footsteps, the bracken smells like burnt sugar, sweet and hot.

Tired from all this carrying, glad for the rest, I sit on the beach beside a windrow of pine needles and birch leaves washed in by waves. My eyes rest on the litter for a long time before they make out a feather the shape of an aspen leaf. Its fringed edge is the color of sunlight on dried leaves, and all the colors of the end of summer mottle its surface: peel of creamy bark, brown alder leaf, golden larch needles under a tree, bittersweet berries as dappled as the forest floor itself. I slide the feather into my pocket. I do not want to lose these colors under the pall of winter.

III.

When the wind picks up, we beach the canoe. Warm enough in the lee of a fallen log, Frank tells the story of himself, a boy tall for his age, who walks in the weeds along an Ohio fencerow next to a field of stubble. He's wearing a canvas coat with a corduroy collar—yellow-brown, like the dried weeds in the fields and the tops of teasels that catch at his sleeve. He's holding a shotgun diagonally across his body, one hand under the barrel, a hand on the stock. Moving cautiously, he waits for the sudden lift of a pheasant in a swirl of wind—a flurry he fully expects and can never be prepared for.

As he steps over a fallen fence post, he spots a pheasant crouched low in the grass, its head down, holding. It's so close he thinks he could grab it. One quick lunge and he has it by the tail. In a great commotion of wings and wind and noise, the bird leaps. Then it's sailing on set wings into the brush. In his out-stretched hand, the boy holds a single tail feather. Long, stiff, the feather is the color of weeds, the canvas coat, the fields, the tops of teasels.

IV.

In a shallow bay on the far side of the island is a tall jack pine with the top broken off. Ospreys have built a nest there, where they can see smallmouth bass in the shadows of floating islands and young pike in the algae beds. When we swing the canoe into the mouth of the bay, an osprey hops to the edge of the nest and starts to yelp. Even this late in the season, she claims the bay as her own, and when she spreads her wings and leaps into the wind to screech over our heads, we decide not to contest the claim. We pull back and bring out binoculars.

The nest is a great mass of sticks heaped on the radiating spokes of broken branches. I can make out a length of pink surveyors' tape, some sticks with dried leaves still on them. And built into the structure of the nest, bracing a layer of twigs, is the entire wing of an osprey.

The wing is huge in my binoculars, a fan of long feathers splayed down the side of the nest. The feathers are brown and shiny, built for strong flight, strong enough to lift an osprey over the lake, strong enough to stand the shock of a headlong dive into hard water, to rise flapping out of the bay and raise both bird and struggling fish.

When the wind rises, the wing lifts and tugs against the tangled sticks, as if it would take flight. On this bright, cold day, the air has an edge I have not felt before. We paddle hard, pushed by wind across glittering water, and skid around a point into a cattail marsh. The wind turns over the birch leaves. They rustle with the sound of falling water.

V.

Some years ago, a cardboard box came in the mail for our son. He slit open the tape and folded back the flaps. "I don't need these anymore," his grandfather wrote. "So maybe you can use these feathers to tie trout flies of your own." Reaching in, Jonathan pulled out a handful of feathers. Peacock tail feathers and ostrich hurl, grizzly hackle, dun hackle, Chinese saddle-hackle, marabou in circus colors—pink, yellow, black, orange. The smell of mothballs and bird skins filled the room. He opened the lid of a plastic box: soft, finely crosshatched feathers from the flank of a wood duck.

He looked up from the feathers. "How can Papa give these away?"

Jonathan knows his grandfather as a surgeon who ties beautiful little dry flies, using all the care he would take with a patient's heart, tying the knots with a sure hand. And now, to give it all up? It's hard for a young man to figure. But the feathers! He dives his hand back into the box. White-spotted hackle of guinea hen. Breast of grouse, brown and speckled. Small feathers from heads of golden pheasants. Gray mallard quills. Spotted pinfeathers from a starling's breast. Coverts from a pheasant's tail.

VI.

Nudged up against the shore of the lake where we've camped, a massive log rocks gently in soft swells. It must have washed up years ago and weathered for many winters, because it's silvery gray by now and splintered along all its seams. I pass the log every time I come to the lake for water, morning and evening for several days.

One morning, when I come down to the water, the log is cloaked in eiderdown. All across its broad back, soft, white feathers flutter in the light. What had been a log has become something else, whispering and lively. It stops me in my tracks.

I imagine a hawk flapping to the log with a young gull sagging from its fists. Holding the bird under one claw, the hawk yanks out beakfuls of downy breast feathers and tosses them over his shoulder. Soon the breast is bare and the next probe of the beak enters the heart. Feathers, pushed by the wind over the surface of the old log, catch in the weathered cracks and tangle in the lichens, riffling, until the log becomes a thing alive again, cloaked in white down, poised in the wind, silvery, fluttering, trembling to be airborne, rocking against the shore.

VII.

Beyond the roll of waves floats what I am quite sure is an eagle's feather. I am afraid to take the canoe out in that bright a wind, but I think if I am patient, the waves will bring the feather to me. How hard it is to wait. The feather rises with each wave, edges closer to shore, then slides back as the wave recedes, gradually rocking toward land. In the end, I wade in as far as I dare and scoop it in Frank's fishing net. It's a flight feather, longer than my forearm. The feather is glossy brown, snowy toward the quill. I run my fingers along the edge, locking each barb in place. Of course, I want to keep the feather. It might still be a criminal offense to keep an eagle's feather, but should I throw this power back onto the waves?

Unsure, I weave the pinion into the lacings of the canoe, where not even the wind can take it. It might be a talisman, some magic that holds on to summer, to memories, to *all these colors*, everything I care about. All this caring. All this keeping. The whole world stretches for flight, and I'm holding on as if for my very life.

"Lay it all down / when you can't hold it," my friend Libby Roderick sings. "Let it all fall / set it all free." Every yearning for friends who have passed away. Every way things might have been different, and every glorious way things once were and might be again. Every spring, sere now and turned to brown.

Every summer, almost gone. Everything that trembles to be gone. Ashes. Ashes. Let it all go.

Drop the feathers into the current one by one. The ruffed grouse. The loon's cry. The urgency of an osprey. Set them adrift. Let currents push them away from shore. Or set them on fire and shove them out to sea. Let them all go. The eagle's pinion, the possibility of strong flight, let it go.

I lie across a bridge that smells of creosote and dried grass. Rough boards press into my legs. The timbers are warm under my belly. Sun falling through alder leaves lights my outstretched arm. I drop another feather. Another. Over the pebbles, feathers bob in quick water, pausing to pivot against a stick, touching a raft of autumn leaves—all the yellows of alder, aspen—slowing in shallows, nosing into shore, darting across the current as if propelled by paddling feet. It is very beautiful, the way water carries a feather. Let it all go. Let it float to the sea.

Acknowledgments

I am grateful,

first and forever, for Frank Moore, my husband, my steersman, my harbor.

for our children—Jonathan Moore, an aquatic ecologist, and Erin Moore, an architect—who tell me what I need to know about salmon in rivers and places in time, about what is beautiful and true, about nourishing love. I'm grateful for their partners, Sue Johnson and Chris White, and for Zoey and Theo, the grandchildren they have brought into our lives. If I care so much about the world, it is for these little children, their hope for the future, and their delight in owls and stones.

for the example, friendship, and very real help of my writing friends, brilliant and generous people—Alison Deming, John Keeble, Hank Lentfer, Michael Nelson, Libby Roderick, Scott Russell Sanders, Carolyn Servid, Mary Evelyn Tucker, Alan Weisman, and especially for the integrity and advice of the members of my writing group, Charles Goodrich, Mary Morris, Steve Radosevich, and Gail Wells.

for my sisters, Nancy Rosselli and Sally Swegan, who are always in my heart and on my mind. I am grateful for the beautiful families of Franz Dolp, Jack Dymond, Alexie Menge, Allen Throop, and Pam Troxell.

for the generosity and steadfastness of the Shotpouch Foundation. For the good work of the Orion Society and the Island Institute. For my students at Oregon State University.

for Carol Mason, who helps me in every way. For Laura Blake Peterson of Curtis Brown, an honorable matchmaker and affirming friend. For Jennifer Urban-Brown, Shambhala editor with an insightful mind and supporting spirit.

for the pond and the island and the valley and the inlet; for this Thursday morning and a Bewick's wren in the hedge.

Notes

Book Epigraph

Rachel Carson, *The Sense of Wonder* (New York: HarperCollins, 1965), 87.

The Solace of Snakes

Frank's colleague who studies snakes in Manitoba is Robert Mason, Department of Zoology, Oregon State University. To read more about his work, go to http://oregonstate.edu/~masonr/.

Burning Garbage on an Incoming Tide

After we witnessed the whales feeding on herring, Frank and I headed for the village harbor, nosing up under the bow of the *Evolution*, the Alaska Whale Foundation's research vessel. The ship had been out in the strait, where scientists attached minicameras to the foreheads of humpbacks so they could photograph bubble-net feeding from a whale's point of view.

When a pod of whales spots a school of baitfish, the whales separate, each to its own job. One or two whales swim in a broad sweep underwater, maybe a hundred feet deep, exhaling a stream of bubbles from their blowholes. The bubbles rise into a curved white wall. Another whale, on the far side of the herring, begins its trumpeting feeding call. This stuns and panics the herring, who flee but find their way cut off by the confusion of bubbles. As the herring mill around in tighter and tighter circles, the exhaling whales complete the circle of bubbles around them, enclosing the school in a net of effervescent water.

Then, from the bottom of the column, the whales unhinge their jaws and launch straight up through the fish. Their gapes fill with water and herring, swelling pouches in their lower jaws like pelicans. On the surface, each whale clamps shut its mouth and forces water through the fringe of baleen that hangs from its upper jaw. Water geysers form between its jaws while, unseen inside, hundreds of herring tumble against the baleen, bounce off the whale's enormous tongue, and slide down its gullet. What had stopped us was the disturbance of giant globes breaking and water lifted by the onrushing whales.

The Happy Basket

The epigraph is from "Is That What You Really Want?" a song by Libby Roderick, from her album *Thinking Like a Mountain*. Words and music © 1990 by Libby Roderick Music (www.libbyroderick.com), Turtle Island Music, Inc., administered by BMI.

Dog Salmon Moon

The end quote is from Rachel Carson, *The Sea Around Us* (New York: Mentor Books, 1961), 196.

Crossing the River

The epigraph is from David Whyte, "The Well of Grief," in *Close to Home* (Langley, Wash.: Many Rivers Press, 1992). I found this poem among the papers left by oceanographer Jack Dymond, who drowned in the Rogue River in 2003.

Overnight Fog in the Valley

The epigraph comes from William Stafford, "Assurance," in *The Way It Is: New and Selected Poems* (Saint Paul, Minn.: Graywolf Press, 1998), 153.

Winter Prayer

The quote from Alain on page 64 ("Prayer is when the night falls over thought.") is cited in the French philosopher Albert Camus's collection of essays, *The Myth of Sisyphus* (New York: Knopf, 1955), 65.

Never Alone or Weary

The full version of the quote on page 68 is, "Those who dwell, as scientists or laymen, among the beauties and mysteries of earth are never alone or weary of life," by Rachel Carson in *The Sense of Wonder*.

Winter Geese in a Green Field

People who want to read Thomas Hobbes should start with *Leviathan* (New York: Penguin Books, 1968), especially part 1 (Of Man). The quote on page 73 ("Things fall apart; the center cannot hold.") is William Butler Yeats from "The Second Coming," st. 1. The end quote is Rachel Carson, from *The Sea around Us*, 250.

A Joke My Father Liked to Tell

Epictetus's (c. 50–120) wisdom noted on page 82 ("There is nothing good or evil, save in the will.") is quoted from *Discourses*, bk. 1, ch. 25. Camus's famous statement about happiness quoted on page 82 ("For the first time, the first, I laid my heart open to the benign indifference of the universe . . . [I realized] that I'd been happy, and that I was happy still.") is from *The Stranger*, translated by Stuart Gilbert (New York: Random House, 1956), 154.

Turning Stones

George Berkeley's ideas about existence and perception mentioned on pages 91–92 are most fully explained in *Three Dialogues between Hylas and Pilonous* (Chicago: Open Court Publishers, 1954). If you haven't read John Steinbeck, *The Log from the Sea of Cortez* (New York: Penguin Classics, 1995), you have a pleasant weekend ahead of you. Plato's theory of forms noted on page 94 is explained in *The Republic*, bks. 5–7.

Things with Feathers

Emily Dickinson's famous poem "The Thing with Feathers," on page 98 is poem no. 254 (c. 1861) in *The Complete Poems of Emily Dickinson,* edited by Thomas H. Johnson (Cambridge, Mass.: The Belknap Press of Harvard University Press, 1981).

Morning in Romero Canyon

The quote on page 102 is from Rachel Carson, *The Sense of Wonder,* 101.

Stillwater Bay, Columbia River

For more poems and short prose pieces about the Columbia River, see *River of Memory: The Everlasting Columbia*, edited by William Layman (Seattle: University of Washington Press, 2006).

To Mend a Broken Pot

To find out more about the conservators' work at the Arizona State Museum, go to www.statemuseum.arizona.edu/about/index.shtml.

Repeat the Sounding Joy

Drawing on the Bible, Isaac Watts wrote the words to the Christmas carol "Joy to the World," reprinted here in the epigraph, which has become a Christmas favorite. It was adapted and arranged by Lowell Mason from an older melody that is believed to have originated with Handel.

The Possum in the Plum Tree

The view of the universe presented in this essay was inspired by Mary Evelyn Tucker, a theologian at Yale University, and Brian Swimme, a mathematical cosmologist on the graduate faculty of the California Institute of Integral Studies in San Francisco. They are the founders of the Center for the Story of the Universe. Many of the ideas in this essay I owe to them. Look for Brian's book, *The Universe Story* (New York: HarperOne, 1994) and his DVD series, The Powers of the Universe. Mary Evelyn is the editor of a wonderful series of Harvard University Press books about religion and ecology.

The Time for the Singing of Birds

The epigraph is from the Song of Solomon 2:11–12. The story of the man listening for God on page 149 belongs to the wonderful California poet and wise, funny man Jim Dodge. On page 150 I write, "I want to say that there is a secular sacred . . ." The person who most beautifully evokes the connection of the secular and the sacred, and whose ideas have deeply shaped my own is the late Viola Cordova. See "Living in a Sacred Universe" in *How It Is: A Native American Philosophy,* edited by K. D. Moore et al. (Tucson: University of Arizona Press, 2008).

Look, the Rain Has Stopped

Erin E. Moore and I co-authored an essay, "Six Kinds of Rain," from which these descriptions are adapted. Anyone who would like to know more about my course Philosophy of Nature can find information at www .oregonstate.edu/cla/philosophy/courses.php.

How Can I Keep from Singing?

The hymn "How Can I Keep from Singing" was written by Robert Wadsworth Lowry in 1860. A century later, in the folk revival of the 1960s, Pete Seeger often performed a less religious version.

I wrote this essay during a gathering of writers and scientists on the shoulders of Mount St. Helens for a field symposium, "Catastrophe and Renewal," organized by my colleagues Charles Goodrich and Fred Swanson and me for the U.S. Forest Service and the Spring Creek Project for Ideas, Nature, and the Written Word (www.springcreek.oregonstate.edu). The geologist is Fred Swanson, Oregon State University. Jonathan W. Moore taught me the phrase "biomass disturbance event." The ecologist is Jerry Franklin, University of Washington. The friends who sing amid the wreckage are the essayist Scott Russell Sanders and singer/songwriter Libby Roderick. You must read Scott's book *A Private History of Awe* (New York: North Point Press, 2007) and listen to Libby's music (www.libbyroderick.com).

Let It All Go (Seven Feathers)

"Lay It All Down" on page 186 is Libby Roderick's song, one that always makes me cry. Words and music © 1996 by Libby Roderick Music (www.libbyroderick.com), Turtle Island Music, Inc., administered by BMI.

Credits

"Crossing the River." Adapted from "The Risk Jack Took." From *Whole Terrain: Reflective Environmental Practice* 13 (2004/2005): 48. And "Geese and Crows." From *Good Roots: Writers Reflect on Growing Up in Ohio*, edited by Lisa Watts, 161. Athens, Ohio: Ohio University Press, 2007.

"How Can I Keep from Singing?" Originally published as "In Endless Song." From *In the Blast Zone: Catastrophe and Renewal on Mount St. Helens*, edited by Charles Goodrich, Kathleen Dean Moore, and Frederick J. Swanson, 22. Corvallis, Ore.: Oregon State University Press, 2008.

"Look, the Rain Has Stopped." Adapted from "Six Kinds of Rain." From *Placing the Academy: Essays on Landscape, Work, and Identity*, edited by Jennifer Sinor and Rona Kaufman, 27. Logan, Utah: Utah State University Press, 2007.

"The Solace of Snakes." Adapted from "Rubber Boa (*Charina bottae*)." From *The Southern Review* 20, no. 2 (Spring 1997): 415.

"Stillwater Bay, Columbia River." Originally published in *River of Memory: The Everlasting Columbia*, edited by William D. Layman, 70. Seattle: University of Washington Press, 2006.

"The Time for the Singing of Birds." Adapted from "The Sacred and the Mundane." From *The Pine Island Paradox* by Kathleen Dean Moore, 177. Minneapolis: Milkweed Editions, 2004.

"Winter Prayer." From *High County News* (Paonia, Colo.), February 5, 2007.

About the Author

FRANK L. MOORE

Kathleen Dean Moore lives in a college town at the confluence of two Oregon rivers and, during the summers, in a little cabin at the edge of a southeast Alaskan inlet. As an essayist, activist, and professor, she brings together natural history, philosophical ideas, and creative expression in a search for lasting, loving ways to live on Earth. Of the many books she has written, three are collections of her personal essays about living in the lively places where water meets land—*Riverwalking: Reflections on Moving Water*, a book about rivers; *Holdfast*, essays about the edge of the sea; and *The Pine Island Paradox*, which explores storm-washed islands and an ecological ethic of care. Her essays can be found in many journals, including *Audubon*, *Discover*, the *New York Times Magazine*, and *Orion* magazine, where she serves on the board of directors. At Oregon State University, where she is Distinguished Professor of Philosophy, Moore teaches courses in environmental thought and ethics. She especially likes teaching outdoors—studying the philosophy of nature in the ancient forests of the Cascade Range or exploring the nature essay with students in field workshops around the country. She is the cofounder and director of the Spring Creek Project for Ideas, Nature, and the Written Word at Oregon State. She best loves exploring wild places with her husband Frank, a biologist, and with the young families of their daughter and son.